Amish Quilts
and the
Welsh Connection

Dorothy Osler

Schiffer Publishing Ltd®

4880 Lower Valley Road, Atglen, Pennsylvania 19310

Other Schiffer Books on Related Subjects:

Quilts of the Oregon Trail. Mary Bywater Cross.
    ISBN: 978-0-7643-2316-4. $29.99

Amish Quilts of Lancaster County. Patricia T. Herr.
    ISBN: 0-7643-2017-3. $29.95

*Quilting News of Yesteryear: 1,000 Pieces and
    Counting*
    Sue Reich. ISBN:0-7643-2595-7. $25.95

Copyright © 2011 by Dorothy Osler

Library of Congress Control Number: 2011937953

Designed by Stephanie Daugherty
Type set in Bellevue/Souvenir Lt BT

ISBN: 978-0-7643-3916-5
Printed in China

Contents

Acknowledgments

WHEN A BOOK IS NEARING COMPLETION, it is always a great pleasure to look back on the research and preparation in order to acknowledge with gratitude the many individuals and institutions that have contributed in some way to the final product. First and foremost, I would like to thank the Harold Hyam Wingate Foundation for funding my research travel through the award of a Wingate Scholarship in 2004. Without this award, the detailed research that has gone into this book would not have been undertaken. This 'field-work' research took me both to Wales and to the United States for extended periods and in each country I met up with friends and colleagues who have given freely of their own knowledge and expertise, engaged in discussions (whatever their views on the topic), and not infrequently given hospitality and logistical support. The value of the assistance, encouragement, and information gained in these encounters (and the fun) is incalculable.

In Wales, acknowledgement is due to: Christine Stevens, formerly at the Welsh National History Museum, St Fagans; Michael Freeman and Mary Turner-Lewis, Ceredigion Museum, and Gwenllian Ashley, formerly at Ceredigion Museum, Aberystwyth; Doreen Gough, Quilt Association, Minerva Arts Centre, Llanidloes; Ann Dorset, Carmarthen Museum, Abergwili; Dr Dafydd Roberts, National Slate Museum, Llanberis; Ann Whittall, Welsh National Woollen Museum, Drefach-Felindre; Margaret Bide; Mary Jenkins and Clare Claridge; and staff at the Carmarthen and Gwynedd Record Offices. I must give special thanks to Jen Jones, Hazel Newman, and Janet Bridge at Jen Jones Quilts, Llanybydder for the time and trouble they took to help me examine the collection, and the patience with which they responded to my many queries. In England, too, I was able to access valuable Welsh resource material most particularly through the good offices of Rachel Terry, formerly at the

Resource Centre, Quilters' Guild of the British Isles, and latterly by her successor, Heather Audin at the Quilt Museum and Gallery, York.

In the United States, as ever, generous American hospitality and a free exchange of information was extended from many quarters. In these regards I must thank: Dr Patricia Crews and Dr Carolyn Ducey, International Quilt Study Center and Museum, University of Nebraska–Lincoln; Ellen Endslow and Pam Phillips, Chester County Historical Society, Pennsylvania; Fran Fitz-Kennedy and Chuck Kennedy; Joan Hamme and her husband; Trish and Don Herr; Barb Garrett; Jane Lury and David Hupert; Stephen Scott, Elizabethtown College, Pennsylvania; Julie Silber; and the staff at Lancaster County Historical Society, Lancaster Mennonite Historical Society, and Pequea Bruderschaft Library, all in Pennsylvania. To two individuals I owe a particular debt of gratitude: to Jonathan Holstein, who encouraged this investigation over ten years ago and provided source material that has been truly invaluable; and to Bettina Havig who has always responded so willingly to my many calls for transatlantic assistance from my English home.

For an illustrated book such as this, appropriate images need to be sourced from a variety of institutions and private individuals. The generosity and friendship given by all those approached for images have at times been quite overwhelming. To the following staff from the institutional lenders, and to other individuals, I extend my sincere thanks for the time and trouble they took following my requests: Emyr Evans, National Library of Wales; Angela Goebel Bain, Illinois State Museum; Kathy Jones, Cambria County Historical Society, Pennsylvania; Jeanette Lasansky, in association with Carol Manbeck, Union County Historical Society, Pennsylvania; Menna Morgan, Wales–Ohio Project, National Library of Wales; Jackie Newey, Quilt Association, Minerva Arts Centre, Llanidloes; Elen Phillips, Welsh National History Museum, St Fagans; Janet Price, International Quilt Study Center and Museum, University of Nebraska–Lincoln; Ruth Ann Robinson, Old Line Museum, Delta, Pennsylvania; Michael Stammers, formerly at Merseyside Maritime Museum, Liverpool; Scott Stoltzfuss, Nicholas Stoltzfuss House, Pennsylvania; Patricia Smith, Allen County Museum and Historical Society, Ohio; Kay Studer, Ohio; Mara Jane Teeters-Eichacker and Kara Vetter, Indiana State Museum; and Wendell Zercher, Lancaster County Heritage Center, Pennsylvania. To the private collectors I am truly indebted: to Faith and Stephen Brown for so freely allowing images of their Amish quilt collection to be used following a request from a stranger 'across the pond'; and to Jen Jones and her husband Roger Clive-Powell for once again letting me include Roger's superb photographs of Welsh quilts.

To Jen and Roger I owe more than thanks for access to their collection and photographs. Not only have they have been a constant support throughout the project, but they also provided accommodation in the heart of Wales' beautiful countryside, and some memorable meals around the kitchen table. Dr Sue Marks, together with Jen, read sections of the text and the final book has benefitted greatly from their collective comments for which I am most grateful.

And finally, to my family, whose companionship and patience have accompanied me through the various stages of this long project. I thank Margaret and John for their love and support over the past year (2010) when the book was taking shape. My husband, Adrian, has helped in a myriad of ways. Not only did he pass his critical historian's eye over the whole text, but he also used his cartographic skills to meticulously prepare the maps. His input has sharpened and honed the text and graphics in ways that I cannot begin to adequately acknowledge, and it is to him that I give the biggest 'thank-you' of all.

Introduction

*A*MISH QUILTS HAVE SPECIAL STATUS in American culture.[1] Known to have evolved in Amish communities after settlement in the U.S., they have come to be seen both as a flowering of nineteenth-century American art and as the embodiment of the faith-based values that are perceived to characterize Amish culture and society: controlled order, simplicity of design, discreet ornamentation, and sober coloring. Once regarded as just another form of folk art, the cultural and artistic profile of nineteenth- and early twentieth-century Amish quilts was raised in the 1970s, particularly after the landmark exhibition *Abstract Design in American Quilts*. First staged at the Whitney Museum of American Art in New York in 1971, the exhibition showcased American quilts not as domestic bed covers but as abstract art. It created a sea-change in the perception of the pieced quilt and, in its wake, Amish quilts assumed a new position as minimalist art forms. By the 1990s, they were being described as "one of the finest aesthetic forms in America...curiously prophetic...of a certain phase of American modernism"[2] and had achieved status in American art history as art forms that presaged the modern art movement. However, most art critics tacitly accepted that the plain, reductive style of nineteenth-century Amish quilts arose within Amish communities as a distinct expression of their separateness from other communities and cultures, "They radiate a fierce stylistic distinction, a forthright economy of means."[3] Art critics were not alone in their assumptions of the distinctiveness of Amish quilts; the author and collector Phyllis Haders opened her book *The Amish and Their Quilts* with the assertion, "Amish quilts are now recognized as being unique."[4]

In this book the aesthetic and cultural status of the Amish quilt will not, in any sense, be challenged, but the book will offer a new perspective on the early development of Amish quilt-making and the influences that shaped the Amish quilt aesthetic. Despite the volume of literature on Amish quilts as a whole and the sociological studies conducted about the group, the origins of Amish quilt-making in America still remain opaque. Whilst many of the high-quality illustrated books on Amish quilts make extensive reference to current Amish lifestyles, the character of the nineteenth-century communities in which Amish quilt-making had its genesis remains under-researched. The assumption is made that, in nineteenth-century Amish communities, women learned quilt-making from their "English" (i.e. English-speaking American) neighbors. Bishop and Safanda's comment is typical: "Borrowing the concept of the pieced quilt from the "English," they [the Amish] began to fashion simple quilts in their own style."[5]

The lack of original research into the origins of Amish quilt-making relates, in part, to a common problem faced by so many material culture studies based on historic textiles, where the lack of surviving evidence becomes a serious obstacle in bringing analytical studies to sound conclusions. Textiles do not survive well over time, and bed coverings—if not considered of cultural or personal value—were frequently re-used and eventually discarded. In one of the first scholarly appraisals of Amish quilts, Eve Grannick acknowledged the paucity of evidence for the earliest beginnings of Amish quilt-making and recognized the need for further study. "A more detailed look at the larger American culture of the 19th century and its effect on the Amish… may shed further light on the story of the 19th century Amish quilt."[6] The work of Grannick, and others who have sought to accurately document and critique Amish quilts and to consider their origins, has greatly informed this text and will be fully considered later.

In essence, however, the corpus of work to date has not sought to question the unsupported assumption that the Amish took the concept and designs of the bed quilt wholly from their "English" (i.e. American) neighbors. So why, within this book, is an argument presented for a connection in Amish quilt style that has its origin in the culture of a small national group on the European side of the Atlantic? Why will the assumption that the design aesthetic of nineteenth-century Amish quilts evolved within Amish communities as a distinctive expression of their simplicity of lifestyle and their separation from other communities and cultures be challenged? It might seem presumptuous for an 'outsider'—one who is neither Amish nor American (nor Welsh)—to suggest that the iconic Amish quilt style could have resulted, in part, not from a spontaneous development process rooted in the Amish cultural mores, but from influences beyond Amish culture and indeed beyond mainstream American culture. However, as Hasier R. Diner commented in her contribution to *Strangers At Home: Amish and Mennonite Women in History*, "outsiders have a great deal to bring to a subject precisely because they see patterns that insiders do not see as noteworthy."[7]

This is exactly how and why this author first gave consideration as to whether cultural interaction between Amish and Welsh communities could have resulted in a shared design aesthetic and influenced Amish quilt style. Having researched the traditions of British quilt-making for over thirty years, the in-depth knowledge of the 'folk art' styles and construction techniques in nineteenth-century British quilts, gained by personal study, informed my visual critique of Amish quilts. Recognition grew that, on nineteenth-century and early twentieth-century Amish quilts, there were patterns of style and structure that appeared to relate directly to certain styles of British vernacular quilts, rather than to contemporaneous styles of American pieced and appliquéd quilts. Particular equivalence was found in the spare style, intensity of color, and quilted textures of the wool quilts made in nineteenth-century Wales which—in terms of overall design, use of plain wool fabrics, and elaborate quilting styles—appeared to bear a striking resemblance to Pennsylvanian Amish quilts of a similar date.

This period of primary research in the 1980s (by the author) built upon previous indications about the remarkable similarities between Welsh wool quilts and Amish quilts, and followed the first articulation and documentation of that idea in a BBC television series *Discovering Patchwork*, broadcast in 1977. In the booklet accompanying the series, the authors wrote:

> It is interesting to compare the Amish quilts with [a Welsh quilt] made around 1880 from fine plain wool in glowing red and beige ... intricately quilted ... [.] There was no communication between the Welsh and Amish—their only similarities were a frugal life and strict Non-conformist beliefs. It is fascinating that the design and use of color should be so similar.[8]

Significantly, the BBC producers and the booklet's authors had used North American quilt dealers and collectors, then resident in London, as program consultants.[9] And it was they who made objective recognition of the visual connections between Amish and Welsh quilts when they first came into contact with traditional wool quilts from Wales; in the 1970s, these were still little-known and certainly culturally undervalued (even within Wales). As well as the visual connections, the strict nonconformist faith connection was also noted, but the possibility of cultural cross-over was not given consideration at that point in time.

In 1987, my second book, *Traditional British Quilts*, was published; it analyzed Britain's vernacular quilt-making traditions and the socioeconomic influences on their historic development.[10] Conscious of the visual connections between Amish and Welsh quilts and, crucially, having discovered the full extent of Welsh emigration to Pennsylvania in particular, the possibility of cultural interaction and subsequent quilt design cross-over was given serious consideration. But it was not possible to look more closely into this intriguing possibility at that point in time. In *Traditional British Quilts*, however, a possible connection between the two quilt styles was alluded to, and this did not go unnoticed by one of America's leading quilt historians, Jonathan Holstein, co-curator of the seminal exhibition *Abstract Design in American Quilts*. Picking up on the commentary on Welsh wool quilts in the author's British text, and noting the Welsh quilters' fondness for "red, magenta,

maroon, dark blue, green, purple, brown and even black,"[11] in an exhibition catalogue essay of 1996, Holstein wrote: "These are apt descriptions of Amish quilt color choices, emphasizing clearly an area that warrants further research."[12] There is no doubt that, in the last twenty years, attention has been piqued about the possibility that Amish quilt design had been influenced by Welsh wool quilts. From their respective vantage points some quilt dealers, collectors, and scholars started to query the received wisdom that Amish quilts are a unique reflection of Amish lifestyles, and recognized the questions that need to be answered.

Though the idea of a connection between Amish and Welsh quilts was sparked by the visual evidence within the quilts themselves, my 'outsider' perspective also recognized commonalities of lifestyle, culture, and emigration history. Wales is part of the United Kingdom, but it is a separate country—the Principality of Wales—with a firm national identity, a distinct culture, its own language, and (since 1999) its own government. In large parts of Wales, Welsh is the first language, not English. Having lived close to Wales and spent time in that country both personally and professionally, I had first-hand knowledge of the country and understood the cultural and faith influences that impacted on Welsh identity. Having also worked in a cultural capacity in Liverpool, Britain's main emigration port to the U.S. in the nineteenth century (and geographically very close to Wales), my understanding of Welsh history and Welsh migration to America was an informed one. And having undertaken one of the most extensive studies of British quilt-making styles and construction techniques, I had a continuously expanding frame of reference that encompassed global quilt-making styles, including those of the Amish.

This detailed 'Old World' knowledge only strengthened the emerging hypothesis that the visual connections between Amish and Welsh quilts were more than mere coincidence and could not simply be explained by the spontaneous and unconnected development of a similar design style within the two cultures. Whilst spontaneous parallel development is theoretically possible, and has undoubtedly happened as cultures respond to similar pressures or stimuli, there were previously un-researched correlations between the Amish and Welsh that went beyond the visual evidence in the quilts themselves. Both cultural groups were underpinned by a strongly conservative Protestant ethic; how significant were the shared strictures of these nonconformist beliefs? If, as will be shown, more Welsh immigrants settled in Pennsylvania and Ohio than in other states in the U.S., how closely connected were the Amish and Welsh communities in the nineteenth century in those states? If they could be shown to have been closely contiguous in time and place, was there evidence to suggest that this could have resulted in cultural interactions that led to the cross-over of design and technique in relation to quilt-making?

To answer these questions, a working hypothesis was developed: that quilt-making evolved in Amish communities in America at some point in the early to mid-nineteenth century, influenced in part by the quilt-making traditions of nineteenth-century Welsh immigrants who settled in neighboring communities. The resultant study focused on finding evidence to confirm or refute this hypothesis, and the salient information from the research is presented here, together with evidence-based arguments for a cultural interaction between Amish and Welsh communities that impacted on the early evolution of Amish quilt-making.

The study has not been without its challenges. It could never be just an object-based material culture study but required a wider disciplinary framework to identify geographical, social, and cultural links between Amish and Welsh communities. So the research had two distinct phases: a survey of surviving nineteenth-century Amish and Welsh quilts in both public and private collections to identify correlations of style and structure; and a study of documentary evidence, gleaned from both primary and secondary sources, that would accurately reflect Amish and Welsh settlements and lifestyles in America in the nineteenth century and set their respective quilt-making histories in this wider context.

As anticipated, the surviving material culture is not only sparse but often difficult to trace and access. The problems of accurate documentation with quilts are legendary and, as with so many other quilt-related studies, have been an issue throughout. Correspondingly, the historical research has been particularly challenging because of its transatlantic and cross-disciplinary nature, and also because of its gender connection. Quilts are domestic items largely made by women, many of whom will have come into the category of the non-elite; all these are factors that have resulted in a lack of historic scholarly attention and documentation.

There have also been unanticipated challenges in looking at the nineteenth-century history of the Welsh in America, the period most critical to the study. Though recent (late twentieth century) scholarly contributions to migration studies do include data on nineteenth-century Welsh immigration and settlement in the U.S.,[13] Welsh immigration has to a large degree been subsumed within the history of 'English' immigration within America. Though the Scots and Irish were recognized and recorded as distinct national groups in U.S. immigration records, Welsh immigrants were grouped together with English immigrants, and were not differentiated out until 1875. In Britain, this particular national separation of emigration statistics took place even later (1908).[14] On both sides of the Atlantic, this was in part no more than a continuation of colonial practice and a statistical convenience, which recognized the reality that England and Wales had been a governance entity for many centuries. But it also happened because Wales is a small country, both geographically and in terms of its population. Yet its culture, language, and identity are rooted in its Celtic past and differ, sometimes markedly, from mainstream English culture. During the study, it became apparent that this sublimation of Welsh culture had impacted significantly on the examination of transatlantic quilt history, resulting in a general lack of awareness that the Welsh had made quilts that could be recognized by distinctive characteristics of design, structure, and pattern. Even in Wales and in the U.K. as a whole, the quality and character of historic Welsh wool quilts were little known and understood until the 1980s, and even then it took perceptive North American collectors to recognize the inherent aesthetic strengths of these quilts.

Now that a greater understanding of the history and traditions of British quilt-making has spread to a wider world, in part through the acclaim given to the exhibition *Quilts 1700-2010: Hidden Histories, Untold Stories* staged at the Victoria and Albert Museum in London in 2010,[15] the position of Britain's regional quilt-making traditions has made a positive shift forward. From being marginalized in the early twentieth century, both culturally and geographically, they have been realigned to a more prominent cultural position in the twenty-first century. For Welsh wool quilts, there has been a particular shift in perspective because their visual qualities and links to Amish quilts position them, in some eyes, as artistic masterpieces on a level with Amish quilts.

But comparisons of aesthetic merit are for others to discuss. The purpose of this book is to argue for Welsh influence in the early development of Amish quilt-making. However, in setting Welsh wool quilts alongside Amish quilts, and in making the case for Welsh influence in Amish quilt design, this book does not seek to infer that the Welsh alone influenced the evolution and development of Amish quilt-making as a whole. Rather, it will seek to demonstrate that spatial coincidences of immigration patterns, economic and cultural connections, and shared nonconformist faiths were all factors that—almost certainly—led to interaction between Amish and Welsh communities in specific localities in nineteenth-century America, and that the design styles of the most celebrated Amish quilts could well have their roots in such interaction.

1

Amish Quilts: American Icon

*T*HOUGH THERE IS A WEALTH of literature on Amish quilts, on the faith-based culture that nurtured these quilts, and on the connections between the two, the purpose of this book is to look at Amish quilts from a transatlantic perspective and open up a new conversation that connects the celebrated Amish quilt with quilts made in nineteenth-century Wales. But in order for that conversation to begin there needs to be a foundation on which the main tenets of the argument can be developed and understood. Accordingly, the first two chapters of this book examine current perceptions and interpretations of Amish and Welsh quilts, their respective histories and cultural resonances. These opening chapters also underscore issues and paradoxes that later sections of the book will address in more detail.

This first chapter focuses on Amish quilts—but not all Amish quilts. Quilts made within Amish communities have up until now been divided into three groups: the early quilts (pre-c.1880), of which there are comparatively few survivors; the larger group of 'classic' quilts made between approximately 1880 and 1950; and post-1950 quilts. For the most part, it is the second group—the 'classic' group of Amish quilts with their plain, deep-dyed wools or cottons, vibrant graphic designs, and exuberant quilting—that have achieved such celebrated status within twentieth-century American art and cultural history. After 1950, several changes to the style of Amish quilts took place and the 'contemporary' quilts—contemporary in the sense of time rather than of design style—are generally considered to have less aesthetic value. It is with the first two groups, which collectively can be considered as the 'historic quilts,' that this narrative is concerned, for it is only on some of the early and classic Amish quilts that potential Welsh connections can be discerned.

The Twentieth-century Rise of the Amish Quilt

It was only during the last half century that this historic group of Amish quilts moved from a position of relative obscurity to one in which they came to be viewed through their visual aesthetic as vibrant works of abstract art. They now have a deserved place in American cultural history, a history within which quilts as a whole have a notably iconic position. Though brought to America from Europe, the quilt is now perceived as a very American 'thing,' even in those European countries which once had strong quilt-making traditions of their own, including the component countries of the British Isles. A detailed analysis of the transition of the Amish quilt from hidden artifact to national icon is outside the scope of this book. However, the contemporary status of these quilts and the interpretations that have resulted from this position do have a relevance to this new conversation about the possibility of Amish and Welsh links. And, because of the comparison that will be made with the cultural status of Welsh wool quilts, it is appropriate at this point to outline how current knowledge and contemporary perceptions of Amish quilts have been shaped.

It was in southern Pennsylvania in the late 1960s and early 1970s that Amish quilts first came to the attention of the 'outside' world. Only a half-day's drive from New York City, the Lancaster County area of southern Pennsylvania became a 'picking' area for dealers and collectors who came to view Amish quilts through the lens of the contemporary art movement. Those 'old dark quilts' hidden away in Amish homes came to be seen as a visual art form whose aesthetic paralleled the minimalist and modernist movements of twentieth-century Western art. It helped that Amish quilts, especially those from Lancaster County, were often square in shape and not too large, i.e. ideal for the apartment block walls of urbanites. Interest rapidly spread, the enthusiasm for collecting Amish quilts became unstoppable, and prices inevitably rose.

The growth of interest in Amish quilts took place within the context of a general revival of interest in the quilt as both a cultural and artistic form; from North America, this revival spread to the world beyond. Pivotal to the revival and to the rising cultural status of

quilts was one of the most significant quilt exhibitions ever to be staged: *Abstract Design in American Quilts.* Curated by Jonathan Holstein and Gail van der Hoof from their own collection of quilts, the exhibition opened at the Whitney Museum of American Art in New York in 1971. It subsequently toured other venues throughout the U.S. before being shown in Europe. Elements from the original exhibition were then shown in Japan, and the overall impact of *Abstract Design in American Quilts* on the world-wide revival of interest in quilts and quilt-making in the late twentieth century cannot be overstated.

The 'Whitney exhibition', as it has come to be known, was a selection of 60 American quilts chosen not for their crafted qualities but for their impact as abstract art. Holstein and van der Hoof were passionate in their determination to have their quilts seen in a gallery setting and judged as art, not mannered craft. In his engaging and illuminating account of the Whitney exhibition and its twenty-year afterlife, Holstein quotes Robert M. Doty, Director of the Whitney Museum at the time of the exhibition. Doty's comments reveal the level of persistence required to persuade a prestigious museum curator to stage such a show at that time, but they also reveal how Holstein and van der Hoof were connecting with the *zeitgeist* of the contemporary art world.

> When Jonathan Holstein called and suggested an exhibition of quilts...my first reaction was negative. ... But Jonathan is bold, and persistent... and went on to mention their similarities to modern painting. I realized that here was someone who shared not only my passion for collecting but also a sense of the affinities between the ingenious art of the nineteenth century and the intellectual art of the twentieth. ...We both looked at the materials of the past with eyes accustomed to the concepts and means used by the contemporary artist.[1]

The 1971 Whitney exhibition was an instant hit and received glowing reviews. How it changed perceptions was neatly summed up in a review in the *New York Daily News*. "Now, the elegant Whitney Museum of American Art on Madison Avenue has given the homely quilt its artistic stamp of approval."[2] Although

1.1. Center Square wool quilt, Amish,
Lancaster County Pennsylvania,
c. 1895. 78" x 78" (198 cm x 198 cm).
Courtesy of The Heritage Center of Lancaster County.

1.2. Center Diamond quilt, Amish, made by Barbara Fisher of Lancaster County Pennsylvania, c. 1900, 82" x 82" (208 cm x 208 cm). © *From the collection of Faith and Stephen Brown.*

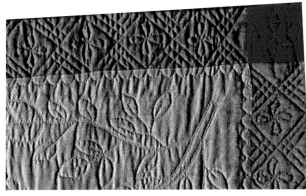

1.3. Center Diamond variation, Amish, Lancaster County
Pennsylvania, c. 1930, 78" x 80" (198 cm x 203 cm).
© *From the collection of Faith and Stephen Brown.*

1.4. Bars quilt, Amish, made by Rebecca Zook of Lancaster County Pennsylvania, c. 1910, 76" x 83" (193 cm x 210 cm).
© *From the Collection of Faith and Stephen Brown.*

1.5. Split Bars quilt, Amish, probably Pennsylvania,
c. 1920, 81" x 84" (206 cm x 214 cm).
Courtesy of the International Quilt Study Center & Museum,
University of Nebraska–Lincoln, 2003.003.0092.

1.6. Sunshine and Shadow quilt, Amish, Lancaster County Pennsylvania, c. 1930, 86" x 89" (218 cm x 226 cm).
© *From the collection of Faith and Stephen Brown.*

1.7. Block wool quilt, Rocky Road to California, Amish,
made by Magdalena Fisher Yoder of Arthur, Illinois,
c. 1910, 68" x 76" (173 cm x 193 cm).
Courtesy of Illinois State Museum.

only one Amish quilt was included in the Whitney exhibition, in the aftermath Amish quilts became a focus of media attention not only because of their visual qualities but, increasingly, because of their connection to the culture and values of an 'other' world, one that held both mystique and nostalgic resonances.

The first exhibition devoted exclusively to Amish quilts was staged just five years later, in 1976, and appropriately was located in southern Pennsylvania (at the Brandywine River Museum), for it was the bold graphic designs of the Lancaster County Amish quilts that were then receiving most attention. In that same year, the first two books exclusively devoted to Amish quilts appeared,[3] although sections on Amish quilts had been included in the new breed of highly-illustrated books on American quilts published from the early 1970s onwards, most notably Holstein's own classic text *The Pieced Quilt* (1973) and Bishop's splendidly graphic *New Discoveries in American Quilts* (1975). Through the 1970s and beyond, Amish quilts became collectable art acquired by both private individuals and public institutions. Some were incorporated into general quilt collections as the cultural (and financial) value of the American quilt increased, but other collectors, drawn to the eye-catching appeal of the Amish quilt, established large collections of the finest examples of the genre. Perhaps best known was the 'Esprit' collection. Based originally in San Francisco, the collection was open to public view whilst displayed in the clothing manufacturer's headquarters, and it was a visual delight to see the quilts displayed on the bare brick walls of an open-plan contemporary workplace. Appropriately, many of the Lancaster County quilts that were housed in the California-based Esprit collection eventually 'came home' when, in the early years of the twenty-first century, they were acquired by the Heritage Center Museum of Lancaster County.

The Lancaster County focus of the Esprit collection reflected the attention that this particular group of classic Amish quilts, made by the conservative Old Order Amish, were then receiving. Of all the Amish quilts, they were the most abstract in form and were visually quite distinctive. The spare style, square shape, Center Medallion format, and fluid quilting designs stitched onto fine wool fabrics differentiated them markedly from Midwestern Amish quilts of the same era. The Lancaster County design formats of Center Square (Figure 1.1), Center Diamond and its variations (Figures 1.2 and 1.3), Bars (Figure 1.4), Split Bars (Figure 1.5), and Sunshine and Shadow (Figure 1.6) became almost synonymous with Amish quilt design, and 'Lancaster quilts' assumed the status of high-value commodities in an increasingly valuable art-quilt marketplace. In 1973, price tags ranged from $350 to $1,200 but, a decade later, sometimes reached $10,000.[4] Though regarded as unique American forms of abstract expressionism, across the Atlantic the minimalist designs of these Lancaster quilts were, in fact, closely paralleled by the structured (if then little appreciated) forms of historic Welsh wool quilts, a connection which will be central to later discussions.

Though attention focused most sharply on the Lancaster quilts, and art critics gave them such critical acclaim, the quilts made in the Midwestern Amish communities of Ohio, Indiana, Illinois, and states beyond also started to attract the attention of collectors. Though using a palette of plain fabrics and darkly-dramatic color combinations, most classic Midwest Amish quilts had been pieced in cottons, not the fine wool batistes and henriettas of Lancaster County. Moreover, for the most part their designs were based on the American pieced block format and used American piecing patterns (see Figure 1.7), some of which were available in printed form from commercial sources.

By the close of the 1970s Amish quilts had acquired cult status—and not just in the U.S. When BBC TV broadcast their 1977 series *Discovering Patchwork*, the British programs and accompanying booklet strongly featured Amish quilts. Not only did the booklet include diagrams of the most celebrated Amish design styles (i.e. those of the Lancaster County Old Order Amish), but its cover illustration featured an Amish quilt design, not a British one! This explosion of interest continued through the 1980s, 1990s, and on into the first decade of the twenty-first century; it has abated little over four decades and has achieved a global spread. The variety of publications on these arresting Amish textiles now ranges from the popular 'showcase' and 'how to' books, through coffee-table art books, historical texts, and books on specific regional styles. The many Amish quilt exhibitions held both within the U.S. and beyond have spawned the publication of accompanying books or catalogs, some of which represent the most scholarly texts on the subject.

From the late 1980s onwards, attention was focused on Amish quilts and their relationship to Amish culture and community through a range of academic filters. But despite the qualitative research and scholarly critiques published over the last thirty years, it has been the provisional assumptions of the early literature that have continued to set the tone of discussion and informed popular understanding. In one of the first books to focus solely on Amish quilts, *Sunshine and Shadow: The Amish and Their Quilts*, published in 1976, the opening paragraph encapsulates the interpretations and resonances that Amish quilts were coming to acquire:

> Amish quilts are now recognized as being unique. Those made prior to 1940 were conceived through the utmost simplification of design elements, simplified to the point of abstraction. Materials were chosen from fabrics and colors acceptable within a community which religiously shunned the outside world. From this narrow disciplined background emerged a distinct and rare color sense. Within the time span of only a few generations this unique form of expression flourished and has since disappeared, perhaps never to return. Such quilts are now sought with the same determination displayed by pioneer collectors of American folk art during the 1920s and 1930s and are being acquired by collectors and museums throughout the world. The territory of the Amish—Pennsylvania, Ohio, Indiana, Illinois, Missouri, Iowa, and beyond—is scoured for the earlier traditional designs. Fortunately it was not always so. Both for the Amish and "outsiders" in what is termed the "English" community, there was a golden age before discovery, a time when quilts were worked in natural materials, dyed with vegetal or European colors, and displayed with a lack of self-consciousness befitting their naive execution...[5]

Other writers in both books and magazines went on to embellish Amish quilt-making with further notions of a self-sufficient textile tradition in which cloth was home-produced and home dyed. True, some of the earliest Amish quilts did apparently incorporate home-woven wool cloths (Figure 1.8), but most classic Midwestern quilts were made from factory-produced cottons. And, though many Lancaster quilts were made from fine wools, careful scholarship has shown that these woolen fabrics were commercially available factory-made fabrics.[6] But once established, such romantic notions are hard to dispel, a problem that bedevils accurate historical analysis of quilt-making as a whole. The notions that Amish quilts are unique, and that their designs evolved spontaneously as an expression of the simplicity of Amish lifestyles and the detachment of Amish culture from mainstream western culture have also permeated much of the literature. Whilst scholarly analysis has demonstrated the significance of the quilt in Amish culture and has examined the associations between the formalized design library and color palette of Amish quilts with Amish belief and custom,[7] the notion that the overall style and aesthetic of Amish quilts are unique remains questionable.

Nevertheless, the academic focus and broader cultural attention to which Amish quilts have been exposed have greatly informed the formal literature, extending historical knowledge and perceptions of Amish quilts, their role in Amish culture and, in turn, their status in American history. Despite this attention, the early evolution and subsequent early history of Amish quilts remain blurred. It has to be acknowledged that there are significant difficulties in developing a coherent history of any group of quilts. Rarely are they signed or dated, and rarely does accurate documentation data or hard evidence of provenance accompany quilts, especially when they become traded antique commodities. Other problems also arise: dates may be inaccurately assigned or genuinely held 'authentic' family histories may later be shown to be inaccurate. The biased survival of artefacts also presents interpretative challenges. Those quilts with high financial or cultural value have a better chance of survival than those of low value, so the broad questions of how representative surviving objects are of their historical period, and what place they had in their culture, are ever-present ones. Then there is the gender issue: because Amish quilts were, and are,

1.8. Detail of Block wool quilt, Amish, hand-pieced with probably hand woven and hand-dyed fabrics. *Courtesy of Illinois State Museum.* (For full quilt see Figure 3.5).

made by women, historical sources that might reveal significant information are limited. And even when accredited historical sources are used as research tools they are still open to misinterpretation; for example, when terminology is considered as possessing its current meaning, rather than its—perhaps quite different—historic sense.

Amish Quilt-making: A Cultural Shift

The difficulties notwithstanding, analyses of historical sources and the surviving material culture have been used by a handful of researchers to investigate the early stages of Amish quilt-making. There is accord that Amish quilts were always made by women and, though skilled needlewomen, they did not bring any indigenous European quilt-making tradition with them across the Atlantic. There is no evidence of quilt-making traditions amongst European Anabaptist groups, nor is there evidence that they arrived on the American continent with hand-stitched quilts in their possession. It is accepted that the Amish, whose spiritual and cultural life was rooted in the Old World, only began to make quilts when settled in America, a world and a culture apart from their Eurocentric origin.

For some considerable time after they first arrived in America in the eighteenth century, Amish households continued to use the feather-filled 'bag', the traditional light and warm bedcover widely used in Europe. (Its contemporary form is the 'continental quilt' or 'duvet' still in use today.) In fact, insofar as historical sources can reveal, the domestic belongings of the Amish who first settled in Pennsylvania differed little from their rural Pennsylvanian German counterparts. In her essay for the exhibition catalogue *A Quiet Spirit*, Patricia Herr confirmed this and illustrated a typical Pennsylvania German bed "dressed as it might have been ca.1800" to demonstrate the style of bed and bedding that was probably used by the earliest Amish settlers before they began to make quilts.[8] In another authoritative account, *The Amish Quilt*, Eve Grannick also made reference to the use of this same style of bedding. She quoted from a treatise on early Pennsylvanian German life which recorded that Pennsylvanian Germans "cover themselves in winter with light feather beds instead of blankets," a clear reference to the continental-style feather 'bed.'[9] So, before the nineteenth century, it

seems that the style of bedding of both Pennsylvanian Germans and their Amish counterparts remained close to the traditional forms of their shared European domestic culture.

So, in turning to making quilts as a new form of bed cover, Amish women made a purposeful cultural shift. Popular belief has held to the notion that Amish women absorbed the techniques of quilt-making from non-Amish (or "English") neighbors, though the cultural mix of these non-Amish neighboring communities is never specified. Whilst the actual process of technical transfer can be explained in this way, the leading cultural question as to why the Amish chose to make this nineteenth-century shift towards an effectively Anglo-American practice is both paradoxical and unanswered. To attempt to resolve some of the uncertainties implied in this shift in Amish domestic practice, scholars turned to surviving documentary sources. In her wide-ranging research on Pennsylvanian and Midwest Amish quilts, Grannick trawled estate records and inventory listings of Amish families in the states that supported well-established, pre-1850, Amish communities: Pennsylvania, Ohio, and Indiana.[10] Her seminal research, and that of other scholars, will be considered further (Chapter 3) when current understandings of the early development of Amish quilt-making will be set in the context of nineteenth-century Amish settlement and society as a whole. At this juncture, however, the purpose of the narrative is to show the context in which the iconic status of the Amish quilt evolved in late twentieth-century America. In this way, comparisons can be made with the analysis of the cultural position of quilts in Welsh culture that follows in Chapter 2.

Once quilt-making had become firmly established as an accepted practice within the cultural mores of Amish society in the late nineteenth century, it moved into its 'classic' period with an exuberant explosion of creativity that lasted until World War II (1939–1945). Amish women pieced quilts in design formats that varied among the various communities and states, according to the liberal or conservative ethos pertaining in individual settlements. Amongst Pennsylvanian Amish communities, quilts made by the Old Order Amish of Lancaster County retained a spare style of characteristic designs based on Center Medallion formats, or broadly-framed block designs, which collectively became known as the 'Lancaster tradition.' By contrast, Amish quilt-makers in the Midwest states used a wider range of pieced block designs, together with different border techniques, producing a style known as the 'Midwest tradition' (see Figures 1.9 and 1.10). Other Amish quilt styles, such as those from the Old Order communities in Illinois and from Mifflin and Somerset counties in Pennsylvania, do not sit comfortably with either of these geographically separate traditions but reflect elements of each (Figure 1.11).

Though the classic styles of Amish quilts continued to be made for several decades as Amish women produced quilts for themselves and their families, once the Amish quilt was 'discovered' by the outside world in the late 1960s, its cultural position changed. Historic Amish quilts underwent a status shift, becoming high-value collectible art and American cultural icons. Sparked by this status shift, contemporary (i.e. post-1950) Amish quilts—though often bearing little resemblance in design or overall quality to classic Amish quilts—became commoditized as souvenir trophies within the framework of an Amish tourist phenomenon, most notably in Lancaster County, Pennsylvania itself. Within easy reach from East Coast urban centres and international airports, the Lancaster County area remains a magnet for national and international travelers alike.

It is, however, the classic Amish quilts made between about 1880 and 1950 that remain as the visual masterpieces of the genre. But the aesthetic lens through which these quilts have been viewed, appreciated and acclaimed, and the cultural signature that the Amish quilt has justly acquired, have unintentionally diverted attention from investigation of the early development of Amish quilt-making, and obscured its relationship to the history and spread of nineteenth-century Amish communities in America.

A Welsh Connection?

As the vernacular wool quilts of Wales reached a wider audience in the late twentieth century, the visual connections between Amish and Welsh quilts, particularly those evident on Lancaster County quilts, piqued the attention of quilt scholars, dealers and collectors on both sides of the Atlantic. Drawing attention to this in a catalogue essay for the 2010 exhibition *Amish Abstractions: Quilts from the Collection of Faith and Stephen Brown*, Robert Shaw wrote:

> While a number of Welsh quilts bear uncanny visual similarities to the bold simple patterns of Lancaster Amish work, it remains unclear whether there is a historical connection, and, if there is, in which direction it runs. The proximity of Amish and Welsh communities in Pennsylvania, however, does make the question of inter-change provocative.[11]

In referencing the visual similarities between Amish and Welsh quilts, Shaw became the latest in a line of scholars to recognize the questions raised by those visual consonances, and to suggest the extent to which detailed historical research would be required to underpin future debate. The first steps in providing the hard evidence that will help answer the question as to whether historical connections between Amish and Welsh communities were possible—or even likely—and in which direction any inter-community quilt-making influence might have run, are contained within the linked narratives of the succeeding chapters.

1.9. Block quilt, Railroad Crossing, Amish, made by Melinda Miller of Walnut Creek, Ohio, 1888, 69" x 89" (175 cm x 226cm). *©From the collection of Faith and Stephen Brown.*

1.10. Block quilt, Bow Tie/Crosses and Losses,
Amish, made by Fannie Yoder of Topeka, Lagrange County Indiana for her daughter,
dated '1875', 64" x 81" (163 cm x 206 cm).
From the Collection of the Indiana State Museum and Historic Sites.

1.11. Center Medallion wool quilt with Evening Star centre,
Amish, made by Anna Swartzentruber Yoder of Arthur, Illinois,
c. 1910, 68" x 79" (173 cm x 200 cm).
Courtesy of Illinois State Museum.

2

Welsh Quilts:
Hidden Celtic Treasures

WALES IS A SMALL, HILLY COUNTRY, bounded on three sides by the sea and only on its eastern flank does it share a land border with England. Though overshadowed and, until recently, governed by its bigger neighbor, the isolating nature of its upland terrain helped Wales retain an independent Celtic spirit and culture, a culture reflected in the quilts produced in this peripheral but beautiful part of Britain. Though the analysis and documentation of Welsh quilts is far from extensive in comparison to the popular and scholarly literature on Amish quilts, quilt-making in Wales has a long history and a particular diversity. Indeed, quilt use and quilt-making began in Wales well before the nineteenth century, but it is the quilts of nineteenth-century Wales that will be considered in this chapter. There is good reason for such a tight temporal focus, for it is nineteenth-century Welsh quilts that have close visual connections to Amish quilts and it is known that Amish quilt-making did not evolve until the nineteenth century. Chronologically, only Welsh quilts taken to the United States after c.1800 are likely to have had any influence on the early development of their Amish counterparts. So, the time frame for cross-cultural influences is narrowed to this crucial century of social and industrial change.

However, in order to explain the visual connections that link Welsh quilts with Amish quilts, the overall context in which Welsh quilt-making developed and progressed requires coherent investigation. Firstly, it is necessary to provide the social context in which to view the development of Welsh quilt styles, and this requires a broad understanding of Welsh social structures pre-1800 to 1900. Secondly, it must be appreciated that Welsh quilt-making did not develop in total geographic and cultural isolation, but was part of an overall British quilt-making continuum. So some specific historical reasoning is required to explain the great diversity and ubiquity of styles and structures that came to comprise the recognizably distinct nineteenth-century Welsh quilt tradition. Lastly, the shifting nature of the textile

2.1. Wholecloth quilt, silk, used in a country house
near Newcastle Emlyn, West Wales,
mid eighteenth century, 72" x 87" (183 cm x 221 cm).
Courtesy of St Fagans: National History Museum, Wales.

2.1a. Center detail of Wholecloth quilt in Figure 2.1.

manufacturing industry of nineteenth-century Wales must be tracked, both temporally and spatially, and considered in respect of its potential impact upon the development of Welsh quilt-making.

Quilt-making in Nineteenth-century Wales: Social and Cultural Contexts

At the turn of the nineteenth century, Wales had a divided social order that reflected its turbulent past. Originally the territory of Celtic tribes, Wales had been conquered and ruled by England for several centuries with its lands divided between wealthy English and Welsh families. By the middle of the eighteenth century these landed Welsh families were effectively anglicized; they spoke English and, for the most part, their faith associations were with the Anglican (i.e. state) Church.

They had large houses furnished in the best of English taste and dressed in fine and fashionable style. The oldest surviving Welsh quilt, the wholecloth quilt from South West Wales dated to the middle of the eighteenth century and shown in Figure 2.1, probably came from just such a landed home and family. In soft and luxurious yellow silk, its sophistication mirrors the refined and often professionally-made wholecloth quilts in use in polite-society residences up and down the British Isles in the eighteenth century. Though only this one Welsh example survives and is now in the collection of the Welsh National History Museum, silk quilts are documented in high-status Welsh homes from as early as 1551, when the last feudal baron of Powys Castle (Mid Wales) had "a qwylte of red silk" in his "New Chamber over ye Garden."[1]

The polite-style of high status quilts was, however, to change quickly with the Industrial Revolution. Britain was at the forefront of industrial change and the British cotton manufacturing industry became a leading player in industrial mechanization and innovation. As a result, new and vibrantly-colored cotton prints flooded domestic and overseas markets, and as well as influencing fashionable dress they also influenced the style and structure of domestic bed covers. By c.1800 making patchwork bedcovers was a popular home-based craft on both sides of the Atlantic; in Britain it developed along trajectories that reflected both class structures and regional traditions. At the upper social levels, making pieced and appliquéd— but unquilted—coverlets remained the preserve of ladies of what would now be called 'middle England', that is, the mainstream of British culture dominated by English metropolitan taste and values. Leisured ladies invested time and energy in ornate appliqué or intricate mosaic patchwork to produce early nineteenth-century 'middle England coverlets' that now, where they survive, evoke much period charm. In the second half of the nineteenth century, the 'English paper piecing' of the middling classes, together with various forms of Victorian fancy work, filtered down the social scale to become the socially-acceptable and taught forms of British patchwork: the 'proper thing to do.'

By contrast, in some of the peripheral regions that were remote from metropolitan influence and had well-established regional identities, quilting (in the strict sense of stitching through layers) remained a key element on quilts, an element that expressed a separateness of regional character and held folk-culture overtones. As regional quilting styles developed and characteristic 'signature' patterns evolved in different areas, it became possible to identify the regional provenance of different quilts on the basis of the quilted designs stitched between the layers. These regional quilts were more egalitarian; in the first half of the nineteenth century they were mainly Medallion (Framed) patchworks of varied complexity, a format that persisted in peripheral regions throughout the nineteenth century, though to a lesser degree as the century progressed. After c.1850, as cotton fabrics became ever cheaper and easy to obtain, many regional quilters chose to invest their quilting skills on the larger canvases of wholecloth or strip-set quilts.

It is in this peripheral tradition of quilt-making that the roots of Welsh quilting culture lay. But, although Welsh quilting shared this common root with other British regional traditions, it evolved some distinguishing traits of its own. Welsh *patchwork* designs as well as *quilting* designs developed strong regional distinctiveness. To a degree, all nineteenth-century British quilt-making traditions shared a common library of quilt top designs. Although specific individual quilt-top designs did evolve in some regions, in general it was quilting patterns and dispositions that became the regional pointers. In Wales, however, it was the generic design format of large pieced shapes joined in balanced geometric symmetry, and quilted in specific regional style, that provided a characteristically Welsh form. And although this pieced format was never entirely confined to Wales, it did come to characterize that country's quilt-making, as did making robust and characterful wholecloth quilts.

Three of the earliest Welsh quilts, similar in style but varied in cloth composition, exemplify this characteristic 'Welshness' to varying degrees and suggest that by the time of their making—the first quarter of the nineteenth century—this identifiable Welsh style had already become an established cultural form. The three quilts do, however, exhibit markedly different characters. Two of them (Figures 2.2 and 2.3) are pieced from fine dress-weight fabrics and are thinly padded, suggesting they were made as much for decoration as for warmth. They do not have quite the vernacular character of the third quilt in Figure 2.4, and more likely were used by those at a middling level in society. Indeed, the dated quilt in Figure 2.2, with '1818' and the initials 'H' and 'G' quilted into the design, is pieced in silk-mix fabrics: two silk-cottons, one silk-linen, and one silk-wool. And even taking into account the fact that some of the individual lengths of fabric are pieced, access to a sufficient yardage of silk composition fabrics for a quilt of this kind would likely have been beyond the purchasing power of a maker from the lower Welsh classes. An additional indicator to this particular quilt's status comes from its fine cotton batting, suggesting that the maker(s) had the monetary resources needed to purchase a commercial filling rather than simply resorting to locally-available, and cheaper, carded wool.

2.2. Center Diamond quilt, Welsh, pieced in silk-mix fabrics, initialled 'H' and 'G' and dated 1818, 89" x 90" (226 cm x 228 cm).
Courtesy of the International Quilt Study Center & Museum,
University of Nebraska–Lincoln, 2006.043.0063.

2.3. Center Diamond cotton quilt, Welsh, Newport, Pembrokeshire,
c. 1830, 83" x 98" (210 cm x 248 cm).
Courtesy of Jen Jones Quilts; photography by Roger Clive-Powell.

2.4. Center Diamond wool quilt, Welsh, Lampeter, Mid Wales,
c. 1800-1825, 65" x 74" (165 cm x 188 cm).
Courtesy of Jen Jones Quilts; photography by Roger Clive-Powell.

2.5. The Principality of Wales.

Surviving examples of early nineteenth-century Welsh quilts are rare, and rarest of all are the woolen quilts from the first half of the century: 1800–1850. Nevertheless, documentary sources are providing increasing evidence that woolen quilts have a longer history and were much more widespread in nineteenth-century Wales than was previously thought. Prior constructs, based largely on post-1850 quilts, proposed that woolen quilts were confined to South and Mid-Wales alone, and that their distribution was directly correlated with the main centres of woolen manufacture in the second half of the nineteenth century (see Figure 2.5 for a map of Welsh regions and for all locations mentioned in this chapter). Increasingly however, the examination of documentary historical sources suggests that such artifact-based constructs give a biased picture, one unintentionally skewed through comparative survival rates. That is, late nineteenth-century quilts are more likely to have survived than those from earlier in the century, whilst quilts of higher social value are more likely to have been preserved than lower-status woolen quilts.

As well as being used in domestic space, Welsh quilts could be found in institutions that were far from homely. For instance, according to records still extant in the island of Anglesey (North West Wales), a payment was made in December 1814 for "a bed and quilt" on behalf of Anglesey's county gaol.[2] Some fifteen years later, in September 1829, more bedding was purchased for the gaol including "carpets, blankets, quilts, bed (covers) [sic] and pillows."[3] No values or descriptions were given for any of the items purchased, nor is it clear whether they were required for inmates or for staff, although the inclusion of carpets suggests that the latter seem the most likely end users. But it seems unlikely that the prison inmates would be allowed the luxury of purchased quilts, even roughly-made wool ones, for on June 1 1816, the labourer Edward Jones had to serve six months in that same prison for theft. And what had he stolen? "One bed quilt made of wool and flax yarn."[4]

Accounts of this kind provide vital clues to the value and status of quilts as well as to their character and material composition. In Britain as a whole, historical court records are proving to be a rich and revealing source of data on quilts and quilt-making. As those at the lower levels of society desperately strove to stay warm, or (less nobly) sought goods that were readily sold or bartered, the theft of bedding of all types was a common crime. Prosecution records can give information not only about the accused, but also about the households from which thefts took place and the victims' status, together with valuations of the items stolen. For example, another court case from Anglesey illustrates the low value that was placed on some early nineteenth-century Welsh quilts; in April 1821, Catherine Lloyd was charged with the theft of "two blankets, a quilt, a sheet and a shift" which had a total value of only four shillings (c. 75 cents).[5] This contrasts markedly with the monetary value of a single petticoat stolen in Criccieth, North Wales, some seventy years earlier. In July of 1755, Lowry Roberts was charged in Caernarfon with the theft of two petticoats; the value of the first, of unknown composition but probably quilted silk, was valued at 51 shillings (c. $13) but the second, a "quilted tammi [i.e. woolen] petticoat" had a value of only 10 pennies, slightly less than a single shilling.[6] Such a fifty-fold difference between the values of the two petticoats is eloquent testimony to the relatively low value of coarse woolen tammy-cloth.

Thus the historical record reinforces the surviving material culture evidence, signifying that quilts were made and used throughout Wales in the early years of the nineteenth century in the homes of both high and low status individuals. Furthermore, the generic design format of large pieced shapes joined in balanced symmetry was in place at least before 1818, the date on the quilt in Figure 2.2. And this design format was used not only to piece the plain-dyed wool cloths produced in domestic-based workshops (Figures 2.4 and 2.6), but also to make high-style quilts in quality purchased fabrics such as colorful printed cottons (Figure 2.7). This generic design style persisted throughout the nineteenth century for both wool and cotton quilts, and eventually carried over into the first two decades of the twentieth century. However, woolen quilts always represented a lower value, both monetarily and culturally, whilst cotton quilts were seen to be more desirable, more decorative and, arguably, were more status-loaded.

2.6. Center Diamond variation, Welsh, c.1850, Cwmsychpant, Cardiganshire, 1825–1850. 75" x 79" (191cm x 201cm).
Courtesy of Jen Jones Quilts; photography by Roger Clive-Powell.

2.7. Center Diamond variation, Welsh,
c. 1830–1840, 89" x 104" (226 cm x 260 cm).
Courtesy of St Fagans: National History Museum, Wales.

2.8. A gathering of Welsh women with treadle sewing machines, c. 1875.
By permission of Llyfrgell Genedlaethol Cymru/The National Library of Wales.

Welsh Quilt-making: Technique and Design

The techniques of quilting—the way in which quilts were pieced, quilted and finished—differed little amongst Welsh quilt-makers from those used elsewhere in Britain. For the most part, fabric pieces were seamed directly together for quilt tops though occasionally 'paper piecing' methods were used for mosaic patchwork centres or for border elements on Medallion (Framed) quilts. Before the arrival of sewing machines as a common appliance in Welsh homes, fabrics were seamed by hand. But the lives of so many Welsh women were tied up with textile production—both for family and community—that they were not slow to recognize the advantages of sewing machines and to adopt them as soon as they became available. In an evocative 1870s image captured by the eminent Welsh photographer John Thomas, treadle sewing machines and their proud owners are set alongside traditional stocking knitters, unmistakably signalling women's textile roles in this particular community (Figure 2.8). In fact, by far the majority of surviving Welsh quilts have been seamed by machine. Once pieced, the quilt layers of top, back and batting (wadding) were set in a traditional frame for quilting. Nineteenth-century Welsh quilts were often made primarily to provide warmth, and so could be thickly wadded with carded wool, blankets or, not infrequently, with an old worn quilt.

Whether pieced in wool or cotton cloth, the design format of symmetrically-organized large fabric shapes gave opportunity for Welsh quilters to display their very considerable quilting skills and to incorporate quilting patterns that, by the early nineteenth century, had evolved characteristic Welsh forms and dispositions. On woolen quilts the quilted lines had to be worked through thick

2.9. This exquisite quilted design on the Center Diamond cotton quilt from
Pembrokeshire illustrated in Figure 2.7 can best be seen on the reverse of the quilt.
Courtesy of St Fagans: National History Museum, Wales.

cloths and dense fillings and were therefore coarsely stitched, usually using a colored thread, but these deeply incised lines produced sculpted surfaces of rich textural quality. On thinner cotton quilts, the softer fabric layers were more pliable, so finer stitching was possible; some of the most intricate Welsh quilting is to be found on cotton quilts. One Welsh region in particular, Pembrokeshire in South West Wales, produced nineteenth-century cotton quilts on which the quilt stitchery is of exceptional quality (Figures 2.9 and 2.10).

Large-scale Center Medallion (Framed) designs, such as the various Center Diamond variations, were not the only quilt designs that were used by Welsh quilters to display their quilting skills, although these Center Medallion designs were inimitably Welsh in style. As elsewhere in Britain, Welsh quilters chose the Strippy and Wholecloth formats for both wool and cotton quilts. Once lengths of fabric had been seamed together for these quilts, the broad flat planes of cloth that resulted could readily be embellished with the structured geometry of Welsh quilting design and

pattern. In addition, Welsh quilters had a repertoire of block patchwork designs and, alongside the more carefully planned and intricately stitched quilts, innumerable scrap quilts were pieced utilizing local wool resources or recycled cotton remnants (Figure 2.11). If quilted, they were stitched with allover or strip quilting designs of simple structure.

The survival of such a range of quilts leaves little doubt but that they were commonplace bedcovers in homes throughout nineteenth-century Wales. Indeed, the very ordinariness of quilts in everyday Welsh life has contributed towards the lack of historic comment on such familiar household objects—a familiarity that breeds invisibility. Only occasionally can brief glimpses be had. Recalling his childhood in the Teifi Valley of south-west Wales at the turn of the twentieth century, the Rev. Daniel Parry-Jones documented the generational transmission of quilt-making and its longevity in that valley. As late as the 1940s he noted that, "Quilting is still carried on in the parish and has come down from mother to daughter."[7]

2.9a. Border detail.

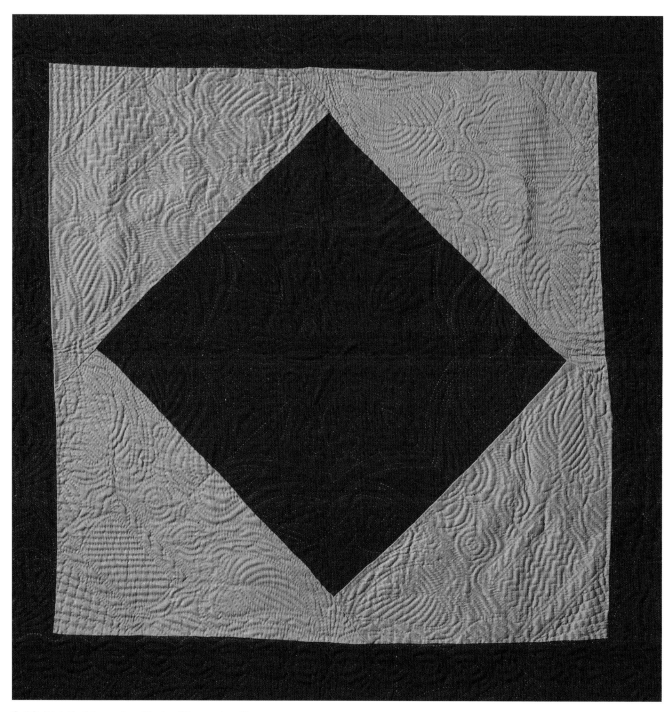

2.10. Detail of the cotton Center Diamond quilt
from Pembrokeshire shown in Figure 6.11.
Courtesy of the Quilt Association,
Minerva Arts Centre; photography by Roger Clive-Powell.

2.11. Wool quilt pieced in tailors' samples,
Welsh, Lampeter Velfrey, Pembrokeshire,
c. 1900. 75" x 79" (191cm x 201 cm).
Courtesy of Jen Jones Quilts; photography by Roger Clive-Powell.

Professional Quilt-makers

Although always a domestic-based occupation, Welsh quilts were also made by professional quilt-makers as well as by those who quilted to provide for domestic family needs. Itinerant professional quilters, usually single women, worked from farm to farm making whatever quilts were required in return for bed and board. They might stay with one household for several weeks at a time, and were familiar figures in South and Mid-Wales during the nineteenth century and even in the early twentieth century. The fabrics required for the many quilts to be made for family and farmhands were brought together at the farm ready for the itinerant's arrival. Quilting frames stored in barns would then be brought out, though some quilters carried their own frames from place to place and some had accompanying apprentices.[8] The peripatetic quilter's financial rewards were undoubtedly low. But the practice provided many a single woman with an income, an occupation in a safe, domestic environment, and a social role in helping to spread news and views, and maintaining inter-community contact in the isolated rural districts of upland Wales. It was a system of social symbiosis that had echoes in other British regions and in other textile traditions, for example, amongst travelling tailors in nineteenth-century Britain.

Other professional quilters worked in their own homes to make quilts for scattered village communities, a practice vividly recorded by Mavis FitzRandolph in her seminal book *Traditional Quilting*, published in 1954, that documented Britain's quilt-making traditions at a time of transition. Describing one Welsh 'village quilter' of the late 1800s, FitzRandolph wrote:

> A certain Mary Jones of Panteg near Llanarth (Cardiganshire), commonly known as "Mari Panteg," who died about 1900, seems to have been one of the most famous of Welsh village quilters and is perhaps typical of them all. Many people in that district still treasure her quilts: she had orders for miles around, particularly from girls about to be married. She lived in a primitive little stone cottage of one storey and worked by the light of a tiny single-paned window. One of her quilts which I have seen, made about 1850 when she was a young woman, is a good piece of work, closely stitched in an elaborate pattern, and was said to be typical."[9]

With a typically Welsh turn of phrase, FitzRandolph was told that "morning and night she was at them," but Mary Jones never had more than four or five shillings (less than $1) for making a quilt.[10] Whether two other village quilters earned any more than that is not recorded, for the mother–daughter partnership of Hannah Davies and Elizabeth Simon is known only from a 1910 image captured by a local photographer. In this rare photograph, reproduced in Figure 2.12, these two village quilters are seen outside their home in Cilgerran, a village in the Teifi valley, the same valley in which the Rev. Parry recalled just such a generational pattern of quilt-making. What kinds of quilts Hannah, her daughter, or the other village and itinerant quilters made is little known, but their concentration in and around this particular valley of South West Wales suggests a connection with the manufacture of woolen cloth. In the second half of the nineteenth century, it was the Teifi valley in South West Wales that became the locus of the Welsh textile industry, the industry to which this narrative now turns.

Welsh Woolen Manufacturing

As the history of Welsh quilts and quilt-making has unfolded, the inextricable link with woolen manufacture has become ever more apparent. From the Middle Ages until the middle of the nineteenth century, the making of woolen cloth represented one of Wales' staple production activities, and the character, colors, and cultural values embedded in Welsh woolen quilts are intertwined with the developments and changes of location that took place in the woolen industry. For over seven centuries, wool cloth was the very stuff of Welsh life; it was made both for home consumption and for sale outside Wales. For the former, it was used in traditional Welsh costume and for domestic textiles, especially blankets and quilts. For the latter, Welsh woolen cloth was exported to the Americas for slave clothing and was bought in large quantities for making army and navy uniforms at home

2.12. Hannah Davies and Elizabeth Simon, village quilters outside their home
in Cilgerran, Teifi valley, South West Wales, c. 1910.
Courtesy of St Fagans: National History Museum, Wales.

2.13. Local women and children outside the water-powered woolen factory at Blaenau Ffestiniog, North Wales, c. 1875.
By permission of Llyfrgell Genedlaethol Cymru/The National Library of Wales.

and abroad. Welsh flannel was widely worn by coal miners and industrial workers because it had a soft, absorbent quality and could be comfortably worn next to the skin; it gained a particular currency for its apparent medicinal properties in relieving muscular aches and pains. In short, the production of woolen cloth sustained a large proportion of the Welsh population up until the second half of the nineteenth century and the spinners, weavers, dyers, and fullers of Wales retained a reservoir of textile skills gleaned from centuries of industrial and domestic practice. Cliché or not, woolen cloth production was woven into the fabric of Welsh life.

Even as early as the twelfth century the Welsh were known as a people with "a wide experience of woollen manufacture."[11] As an adjunct to farming and animal husbandry, they produced yarn and cloth in their own homes for their own use. When a commercial industry developed alongside the self-sufficiency of the original domestic-based craft, some of the processes of textile production became centralized. Fulling (shrinking) cloth was the first process to be taken out of the home with fulling mills (*pandy*) built in almost every village location within walking distance of home-based spinners and weavers. Then, as commercial cloth production increased, craftsmen dyers were needed to produce the variety of colors required for mercantile markets, so that too became a specialized process.

When large-scale water power was introduced into the textile industry in the late eighteenth century, the processes of carding and spinning were increasingly mechanized inside new, purpose-built factories. With its hilly terrain and fast-flowing streams, Wales was ideally positioned to take advantage of this form of natural power (Figure 2.13). Though most commercial enterprises mechanized these processes, where woolen yarn continued to be required for the home production of cloth and knitted goods, home-spinning continued throughout the first half of the nineteenth century and beyond, with any surplus domestic product sold at regular local markets. Describing the sights and sounds of just such a market in Newtown, Mid-Wales in 1801, the traveller Thomas Martyn wrote in his journal, "The women stand with their baskets of spun wool along the street, and in every house the spinning wheel rattles incessantly."[12]

But weaving woolen cloth was still done on hand looms in Wales until late in the nineteenth century, long after power-driven looms had been introduced into cotton manufacturing in northern England and adjacent parts of North Wales. According to official reports of the 1830s, there were still over 3,000 hand-loom weavers spread throughout Wales, working either in single home-based loom houses (known as *tŷ gwŷd*) or else in high-windowed weaving 'factories' stretching across the upper levels of several adjoining weavers' cottages. In this way, and although still not fully mechanized, weaving activities did become part-centralized along proto-industrial lines in the first half of the nineteenth century, particularly in Mid-Wales. It was not until the last quarter of the nineteenth century that power looms were introduced in Wales for weaving woolen cloth. At that point, Welsh woolen manufacture finally became fully mechanized and, as a result, there was a marked shift in the geographical concentration of the industry. Though domestic hand-loom weavers continued to work throughout the country, the previously important commercial centres in Mid- and North Wales withered away in the face of competition from the steam-powered mills of northern England. Inward-looking Welsh conservatism had taken its toll when the industry failed to adapt and, as a result, residual operations became concentrated in the south-west corner of Wales. With its ample supplies of waterpower, woolen manufacturing still flourished in the south west, supplying flannel for industrial clothing, uniform cloth for military markets, blankets (*carthenni*), and the double-cloth 'tapestry' bedcovers that became the high-end product of the automated industry. Surviving woolen quilts wholly

reflect this temporal and geographical shift, with the majority dating from post-1870 and coming from areas not too distant from the Teifi valley, the final focus of this age-old Welsh industry.

Welsh Quilts and Welsh Dress: Inter-relationships of Color and Cloth

Of all the types of wool cloth produced in Wales, it was the clothing flannels that mostly found their way into quilts—hence the much-used term 'flannel quilts.' Welsh flannel became a cloth of high repute; it was produced in a variety of checks and stripes as well as plain-colored cloths in dense, saturated colors. The finer cloths were used particularly for men's shirtings but the full range of flannels had other clothing uses including jackets and trousers for men, and the *betgwns* (cloaks) and petticoats that were essential elements of traditional Welsh dress for women. Throughout the nineteenth century, Welsh women dressed in a common style that became a firm expression of national identity. Probably based on an earlier peasant-style of dress known not only in Wales but also in rural England, the characteristic Welsh form with its regional variations was set in the early years of the nineteenth century, following a national consciousness movement.[13] It subsequently persisted as everyday wear through much of the nineteenth century before being transmuted to 'Sunday-best' and eventually to festival or '*eisteddfod*' costume, which some now regard as pastiche.

Paintings, portraits and monochrome photographs of men and women in nineteenth-century Welsh costume abound. Literary records also provide evocative descriptions of Welsh character and dress, none more so than the famous travelogue of Englishman George Borrow, *Wild Wales* (1854). In one village in North Wales he recounts that he stepped into a small cottage to be greeted by the woman of the house with '*Croesaw, dyn dieithr*' ('Welcome, foreign man'). Welsh-speaking and with little English, she was dressed in what Borrow described as "the ancient Welsh costume, namely, a kind of round half-Spanish hat, long blue woolen kirtle or gown, a crimson petticoat, and a white apron, and broad, stout shoes with buckles."[14] In cameos like this, the 'foreigner' Borrow captured the cultural divide that still separated Wales and its indigenous population from their English

2.14. Lithograph of churchgoers in traditional Welsh costume, c. 1850.
By permission of Llyfrgell Genedlaethol Cymru/The National Library of Wales.

neighbors in the mid-nineteenth century. In *Wild Wales*, the Welshness of those that Borrow encountered shines through his compelling narrative.

Borrow's recollection of a *blue* woolen kirtle and a *crimson* petticoat are of more than passing interest for it is these two colors that are often combined in two-tone Welsh quilts (Figure 2.15). With blue from imported indigo and red from home-grown madder or imported cochineal, they represent just part of the extensive color palette that skilled Welsh dyers could produce. Welsh wools were variously dyed: in the raw state as spun yarn for knitting and weaving, or as woven cloth dyed 'in the piece'. As a highly reactive substance, wool was not difficult to dye and absorbed color well but, though home dyeing was an option, most cloth was dyed by specialized craftsmen with recipes handed down from generation to generation. Only they could reliably produce an evenly-dyed cloth of intense color suitable for markets or other commercial outlets.

The full range of colors that Welsh dyers could and did produce is revealed in fascinating unpublished documents and dye-books now in the National Library of Wales. In one, dated 1794, the North Wales dyer Peter Price announced his intention to record his skills with the inscription: "Peter Price His Book Bought in London May 26th 1767 to rite Down Doiroxiwnee [Directions] for all Sorts of Dein bisness in Silk & Woolin & cotton." His curious English spellings notwithstanding, Peter Price goes on to record pages of detailed recipes for the deep, saturated colors that radiate from Welsh quilts: "Gold... Saxon Green... Cheroy... Crimson... Sgarlet... Pompy Dore... Ripe Aple... Copor Color... Comon Black... Bottle Green... Raven Black... Blew."[15] Handed down through the generations, this was the color palette of locally-produced cloth available to the Welsh quilter. Even after the introduction of synthetic dyes in the second half of the nineteenth century, local recipes continued to be recorded and passed on. Precisely a century after Peter Price had begun his dye notations, another dyer in North Wales was still giving instructions for those two signal colors of Welsh women's dress: red and navy blue (Figures 2.16 and 2.17).[16]

2.15. Pin-wheel quilt in red and blue wool, Synod Inn, Cardiganshire, c. 1875.
Courtesy of Jen Jones Quilts; photography by Roger Clive-Powell.

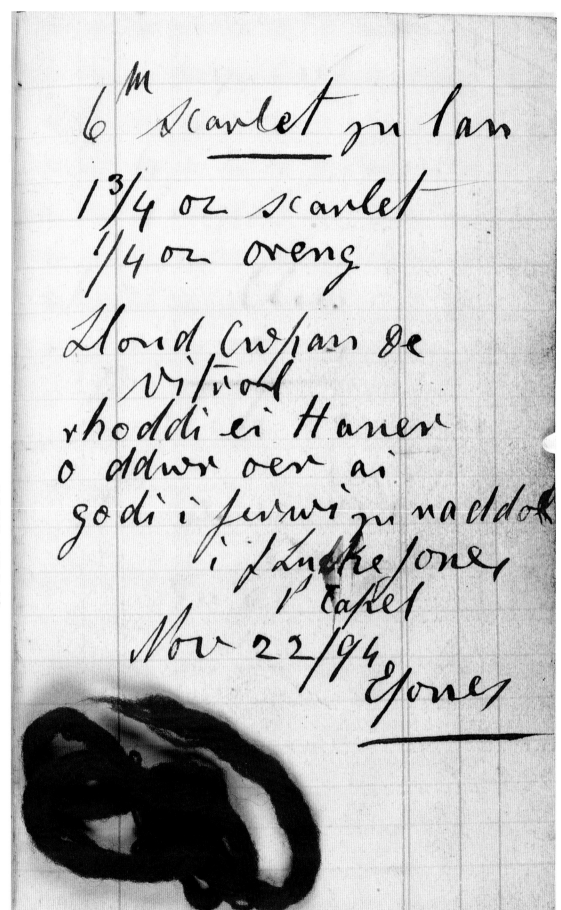

2.16. Page from a Welsh dyer's notebook showing the recipe for scarlet red dye, 1894. *By permission of Llyfrgell Genedlaethol Cymru/The National Library of Wales.*

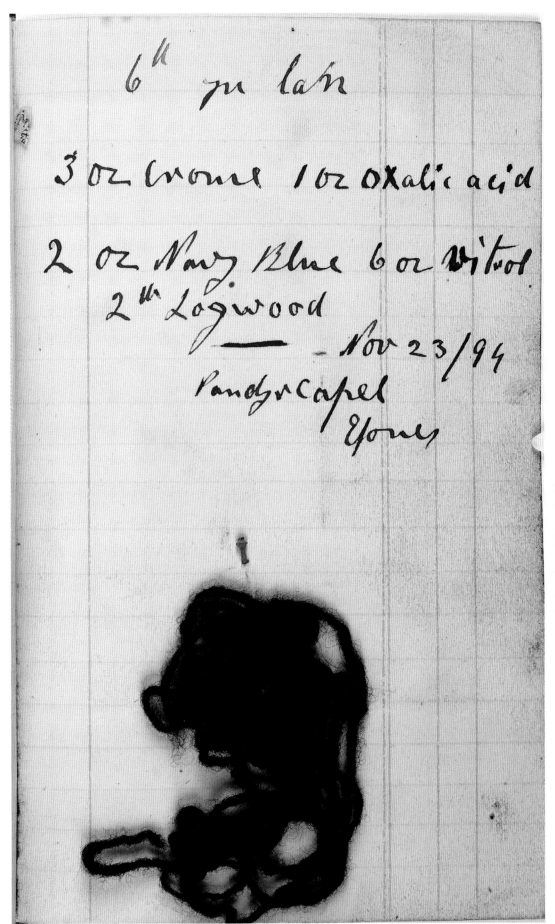

2.17. Page from a Welsh dyer's notebook showing the recipe for dark blue (navy) dye, 1894. *By permission of Llyfrgell Genedlaethol Cymru/The National Library of Wales.*

2.18. Center Medallion quilt with a pieced block center,
Welsh, Salem, Llandeilo, Carmarthenshire,
c. 1880, 68" x 87" (173 cm x 221 cm).
Courtesy of Jen Jones Quilts; photography by Roger Clive-Powell.

Quilts in Welsh Culture

However rich in color, Welsh woolen cloth never had high-fashion status. From loosely-woven coarse '*styff*' (stuff) to fine flannel, Welsh woolens had high value for their practical uses but low value as fashionable dress. Wool became associated with vernacular clothing and therefore regarded as an everyday, low status cloth, warm and practical but with social and cultural overtones that denoted inferior class and place. That same vernacular association was attached to woolen quilts. In a culture where wool cloth was everyday currency, woolen quilts had little value as anything other than warm bedcovers. Only their discovery by astute collectors a century and a half later altered that pragmatic perception. Even some of those quilts that have now been repaired and restored were used almost to destruction, reaching their domestic end as insulation for cars, tractors and even the odd farmyard animal. Amusing tales abound about how these woolen quilts finally came, sometimes literally, out of the woodwork. Only persistence on the part of one collector brought the quilt in Figure 2.18 to light from a dusty garage loft to which it had been consigned for years. Made in the 1880s in South West Wales, its abstract qualities and glowing colors are simply captivating.

However amusing, there is serious point to these anecdotes for they underscore the lack of value given to woolen quilts within Welsh culture itself. The explanation for this is not simply that they were products of a folk culture, for other Welsh folk arts, particularly those crafted in wood, have been invested with national and cultural identity and have been documented and collected by antiquarians and historians for many decades. But quilts were made by women; they were domestic products for private space. Woolen quilts were dark, thick and heavy and, moreover, were made from the scatterings of an indigenous industry that made worthy wools, not pretty cottons. These factors combined to make woolen quilts invisible outside the gender-based networks in which they were made and used, factors that provide interesting parallels with the status of classic Amish quilts within Amish society until the 1970s. Just as in Wales, dark quilts were regarded by some American Amish as old and ugly.[17]

Held in such low regard, few Welsh quilts were collected—either by individuals or by institutions—until the 1950s. Those that had survived were, for the most part, kept in homes for personal and sentimental reasons or for the insulating purposes described above that send shivers down the spines of quilt enthusiasts in the twenty-first century. But a new national impetus came with the folk-museum movement that led to the establishment of the Welsh Folk Museum just outside Cardiff in 1948 (now renamed the Welsh National History Museum). With houses and cottages amongst the buildings recreated on site, there was a need for furnishings in appropriate style. It was initially for this purpose that the museum built up its collection of Welsh quilts, but their value as objects still rested on their association with Welsh tradition, not in their aesthetic, and they remained insignificant within the overall perception of Welsh culture.

It was recognition of the visual connections and shared aesthetic of Amish quilts with Welsh quilts that initiated the change a perception. And it came from without, not from within, Wales. In the more general revival of interest in quilts in the 1970s, it was British-based North American collectors and dealers, some with close ties to Wales, who recognized the cultural and aesthetic qualities of Welsh quilts, particularly the woolen quilts. Some individuals began to build up Welsh quilt collections at much the same time that the Whitney exhibition *Abstract Design in American Quilts* came to Bristol and Manchester. But it is a comment on the extent to which Welsh quilts still remained hidden at this seminal point in time that no voice within Britain's cultural community could point the exhibition's visiting curators to the equally exciting examples of nineteenth-century abstractionism just along the road in Wales.

With the opening (2009) of *Jen Jones Welsh Quilt Centre* in Lampeter, a market town in the heart of Wales, the profile of Welsh quilts has at last been raised and given fitting national and cultural status. Housed on the Old Town Hall of Lampeter, with the beautifully-restored old court room providing lofty exhibition space, the Centre is a fitting home for Wales' most important quilt collection and gives on-going opportunity to showcase this remarkable genre of British quilts.

3

Amish Communities and Amish Quilt-making in Nineteenth-century America

*F*OR THE GREATER PART of the last three centuries, the Amish in America lived in relative obscurity in close-knit communities bounded by faith and community codes. In the second half of the twentieth century that changed as their particular piety, together with their rejection of aspects of technological change, created an increasingly visible separation from mainstream society. As a result, Amish communities became the focus of popular and scholarly attention, whilst their lifestyles and artefacts increasingly became the stuff of tourism and enthusiastic collecting. This attention spawned numerous books and articles, including the comprehensive and authoritative accounts on which this book has drawn. But much of this literature relates to Amish custom and society in twentieth-century America, not that of the previous century. The context of this book requires an understanding of the Amish presence in America in the nineteenth century, a period generally considered to be the least studied part of Amish history. Consequently, this chapter will provide an account of Amish society and settlement across nineteenth-century America, an account that can be directly related to the narrative of nineteenth-century Welsh immigration and movement across America that follows in Chapter 4.

An understanding of the history and spread of Amish communities in nineteenth-century America requires a complementary understanding of the context of the arrival of the earliest Amish immigrants, in the first half of the eighteenth century. The precise date when the Amish first set foot on America's east coast shores is a matter of some dispute, but there is no dispute about why this Anabaptist group came to the New World. They left Europe in search of freedom from the religious persecution that they had suffered in Switzerland and the Palatinate of southern Germany. Like other Nonconformists, including Welsh Quakers and Welsh Baptists, the first Amish settlers

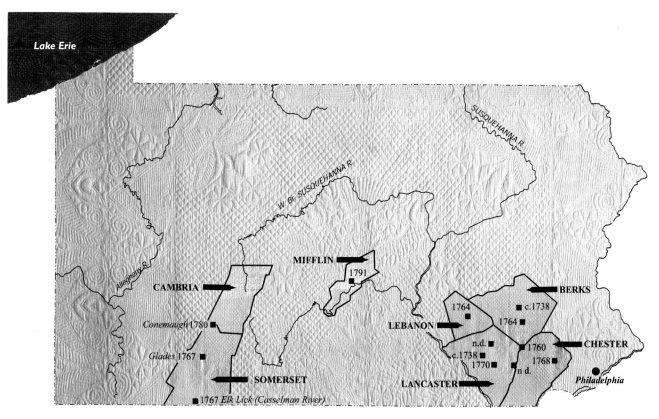

3.1. Pre-1800 Amish settlements in Pennsylvania.

took advantage of the opportunities offered by William Penn's agents in Pennsylvania to purchase land, and thus escape to a colony that had become a haven for minority religious groups.

The initial waves of Amish settlers are commonly believed to have arrived between 1717 and 1750. A total of approximately 500 Amish immigrants arrived during that period, establishing settlements in southeastern Pennsylvania. The first such settlements were in Berks County, quickly followed by others in Lancaster and Chester counties (see map in Figure 3.1). The 150–200 Amish settlers of Berks County helped pioneer the area as a component part of a larger group of German farmers, most of whom apparently prospered.[1] But conflict with Native Americans and loss of soil fertility became concerns; one settlement had died out by 1786 and the surviving families moved into the Conestoga Valley of Lancaster County. The other Berks County settlement continued into the 1830s, a decade that also saw the demise of the Chester County community after its members moved on.

When the Amish pioneers from the failed Berks County settlement moved into the Conestoga Valley

they occupied land that had originally been acquired and farmed by Welsh settlers. In his account of the first Amish settlements in America, Grant Stoltzfus recorded this transfer of land directly from the Welsh to the Amish:

> On these large tracts of land drained by the Conestoga Creek, these Welsh settlers built homes, erected forges and mills, and tilled the soil. At one end of the valley, they erected the Bangor Episcopal Church in what is now Churchtown... At the other end of the valley they built St Thomas Episcopal Church in the present town of Morgantown... Nearly all the land and homes of the Welsh have passed from their hands into those of the Amish.[2]

This change in land ownership began around 1760. The Welsh settlers who sold their land to the Amish at that time were descendants of the Welsh Quakers and Baptists who had left Wales in the seventeenth century, affinity groups who had emigrated from Wales for much the same reason

3.2. Drawing by Roger Cooke of the restored homestead of Nicholas Stoltzfus
and his descendants at Wyomissing, near Reading, Pennsylvania;
Nicholas was an Amish emigrant from Germany who arrived in Philadelphia in 1766.
Courtesy of the Nicholas Stoltzfus House Preservation Committee, nicholasstoltzfus.org.

as the Amish had left Europe—to escape religious persecution. However, despite their geographic connection and economic interaction, these Welsh settlers were unlikely to have had any influence on the development of Amish quilt-making, for they had reached America long before the evolution of those vernacular Welsh quilt-making styles that bear such close comparison to Amish quilts.

From their new base in the upper Conestoga Valley, the Lancaster County Amish expanded southwards in the early nineteenth century, occupying the Mill Valley and Pequea Valley areas—locations closer to the Susquehanna River. Despite fluctuating numbers and the fragmentation that occurred in the 1860s as more liberal elements joined other Anabaptist groups, the conservative arm of the Lancaster Amish community retained a presence in the area that lasted throughout the

rest of the nineteenth century and continues to the present day. In the second half of the nineteenth century this community came to be known as the 'Old Order Amish', and it was they who produced the celebrated classic Lancaster Amish quilts.

As new frontier lands were opened up at the close of the Revolutionary War (1783), some Amish communities took the opportunity to move westwards from their existing settlements in south-eastern Pennsylvania. Nevertheless, the first of these new western settlements, or 'daughter colonies', were still within the bounds of Pennsylvania. Somerset County in west-central Pennsylvania was first settled by the Amish in 1767, two years before the area was officially opened up for occupation,[3] and the first Amish families to buy land in the Big Valley area of Mifflin County, central Pennsylvania, arrived in 1791–93. Although Amish groups moved into other areas of Pennsylvania at that time (e.g. Union County), the Somerset County and Mifflin County groups were the most prominent of all. Correspondingly, as the nineteenth century progressed, the original south-eastern Pennsylvanian settlements proved to be remarkably stable in respect of settlement continuity, with only a few scattered families moving on, despite the fact that this same area had been the springboard for westward Amish migration in the eighteenth century.[4]

Though less well recognized in Amish quilt literature, those Somerset County settlements that had been formed in the late eighteenth century came to hold a particular significance in relation to Amish–Welsh connections. Although often referred to as a single 'Somerset County' settlement, there were in reality three communities or congregations running in a near north-to-south line: the Conemaugh congregation in the north; the Glades congregation in central Somerset County; and the Elk Lick (or Casselman River) congregation in the south, this last close to the Pennsylvania–Maryland border. Though comprising three separate communities, all were linked by ministering church leaders and bishops. However, only the Elk Lick congregation survived into the twentieth century.

Even though it did not survive as long as Elk Lick, the original Conemaugh congregation is of particular interest. Located around what is now Johnstown, a settlement that was founded by the Amish pioneer Joseph Shantz (anglicized to 'Johns'), Conemaugh's location was not entirely within Somerset County but also included the southern part of what, in 1804, became Cambria County, so-named because of the Welsh immigrants who arrived there in 1796 (*Cambria* is the Latin word for Wales). Of this area, Alvin Beachy records that:

> The Amish were in Johnstown and its vicinity in sufficient numbers to give their name [Yoder] to one of the city's suburbs. Even after the congregation became almost extinct, this suburb was known for a long time as "Der Amish Hivel", because at one time it was practically all owned by Amish people."[5]

The dominance of the Amish on the Cambria County/Somerset County border in the early nineteenth century is confirmed by contemporary census records. In the 1800 census, when the whole area was still Somerset County, approximately 60% of the total population had names with Amish associations.[6] Twenty years later, in 1820, the section that was by then in Cambria County still retained a similar proportion, although overall numbers had dropped by about 20%. The 1850 census, however, shows that the Amish character of the community had markedly changed; only 14% of the population in the Cambria County section now had potentially Amish names, although the figure in the Somerset County section was significantly higher at 35%.[7]

Two things were apparently happening in Somerset County in the first half of the nineteenth century. Firstly, there was some fluidity between the congregations. Secondly, and significantly, families from Somerset County settlements were following the pioneer route west. According to Beachy:

> The Amish pioneers in Somerset County were a restless lot. The virgin forest of the Somerset County hills had scarcely been brought under cultivation when these pioneers were on the march again, this time westward into the Ohio Territory.[8]

The flatter and more fertile lands to the west proved attractive to Amish pioneers from Somerset County, as the map of Amish westward movement in Figure 3.3 shows. In 1808 and 1809, families from the Elk Lick congregation moved to settle in Ohio, in Holmes County and Tuscarawas County, then expanded into nearby counties to form the basis of what became, and still is, the largest single Amish settlement in America. Some thirty years later, in 1842, a group from the Conemaugh congregation settled in Elkhart County, Indiana, expanded into Lagrange County and eventually formed the largest single congregation west of Ohio. Then, just three years later, in 1845, a major leap took place as two Amish groups from Somerset County moved through Ohio, Indiana, and Illinois to settle in

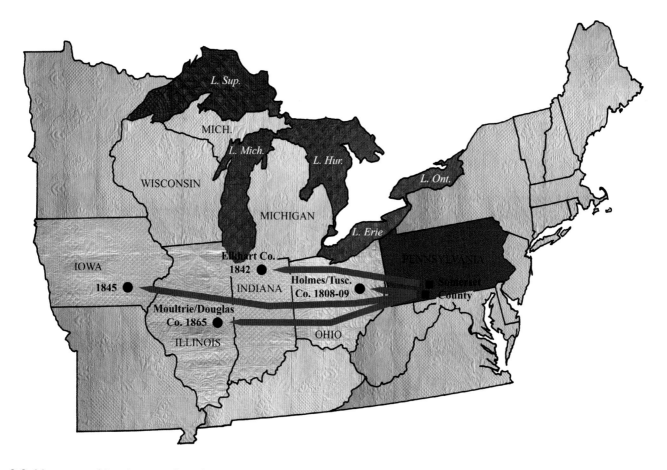

3.3. Movement of Amish groups from Somerset County, Pennsylvania to the Midwest states: 1800–1850.

Iowa. Though new Amish immigrants had settled in central Illinois in the 1830s, it was not until 1865 that families from Somerset County settled there, when a group from the Elk Lick congregation started the community around Arthur, in central Illinois. It is from this Moultrie/Douglas Old Order Amish community that some of the earliest Amish quilts have come; Illinois quilts dated to 1850–70 are shown in Figures 3.4 and 3.5. Since this community was not established until 1865, there is a strong possibility that these quilts were actually brought to Illinois from Somerset County but, if not, then the quilt-making skills that went into their making could have been taken there by members of the migrating community from Pennsylvania. These wool quilts, now in the Illinois State Museum collection, may well represent examples of the earliest phase of Amish quilt-making.

The communities of west-central Pennsylvania were undoubtedly pivotal in the migration of the Amish into the Midwest and, in the summation of his work on the 'Somerset County' settlements, Beachy emphasizes that:

> The capacity for the Somerset County Amish for pioneering was truly remarkable. When it is remembered that their pioneering days lasted for more than half a century, 1808 to 1865, during which time the Somerset County Amish were pioneers in Ohio, Indiana, Iowa, and Illinois, the wonder is not that two congregations in Somerset County should have become extinct, but rather that any should have survived.[9]

The Somerset County Amish were not the only mother communities for the movement west. Families from the successful groups established in Mifflin County's Big Valley also moved into Ohio, with subsequent daughter colonies settling in Missouri and Oregon. But from about the 1820s

3.4. Block wool quilt, Nine Patch, Amish, hand-pieced by Catherine Beachy Kaufmann
between 1850 and 1870 and subsequently used as the filling for a comforter;
Catherine came to Illinois in 1868, 66" x 79" (167 cm x 200 cm).
Courtesy of Illinois State Museum.

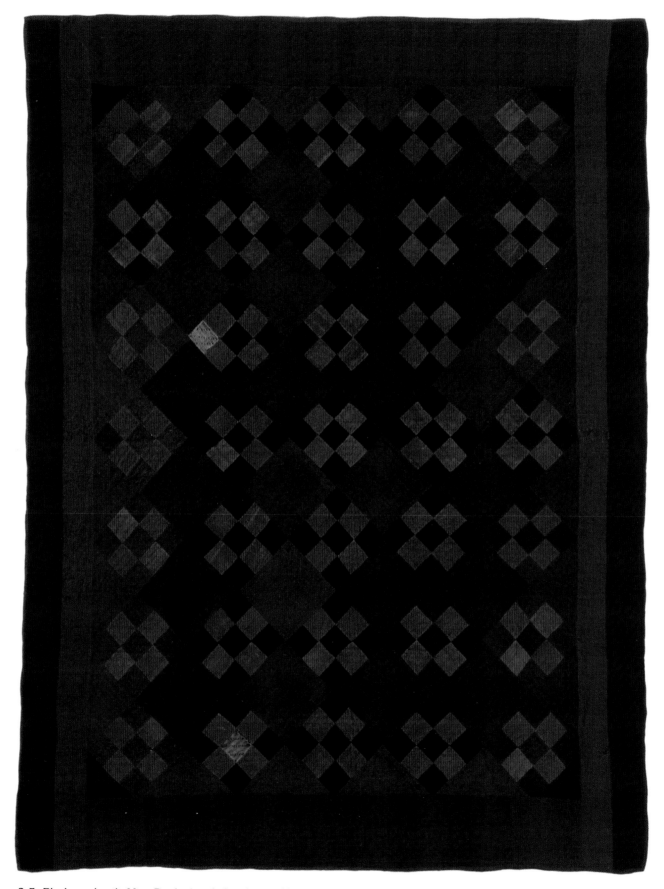

3.5. Block wool quilt, Nine Patch, Amish, hand-pieced by Barbara Yoder Otto between 1850 and 1870; Barbara was one of the first Amish women to settle in Douglas County, Illinois in 1865, having been born and married in Somerset County, Pennsylvania, 62" x 80" (157 cm x 203 cm). *Courtesy of Illinois State Museum.*

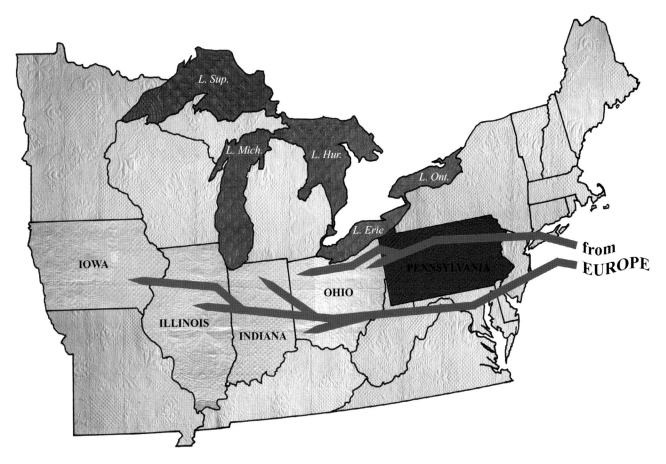

3.6. Nineteenth-century movement into Midwest states by Amish immigrants from continental Europe.

onwards new Amish immigrants began to arrive from Alsace and, a decade later, from the Hesse area of Germany too (see chart in Figure 3.6). Searching out inexpensive land, some moved directly into the Midwest states, either joining established settlements there or forming new communities such as those in central and southwest Ohio (on the fringes of Holmes County and in Butler County, respectively).[10] As the historical geographer William J. Crowley records, these new communities were generally more progressive in attitude:

> Colonies founded exclusively by Alsatian Amish did not survive as [Old Order] Amish settlements beyond about 1870. In many cases the people moved elsewhere, and in other instances they joined more progressive Mennonite bodies. While their Amish brethren who had come to the United States in the first wave [of Amish migration] remained little changed, the Alsatians ... found the resident

Amish in the United States too conservative. The Amish arriving from the German areas were ... less progressive than the Alsatians and their survival rate as Old Order Amish was significantly higher. All of the [Alsatian] settlements made in Illinois ... all but one in Iowa, and all but one in Ohio eventually failed ...The one area of significant deviation from this trend was in northeastern Indiana, where five colonies survived to the present.[11]

Crowley's evidence indicates that the divisions that were to splinter the Amish church in the 1860s were already beginning to be felt between established communities and new immigrants even as the westward migration progressed. After the 1860s this westward advance slowed, though by then it had extended into the Great Plains and beyond. However, very few new Amish immigrants arrived in America after 1860, and all the new settlements that were subsequently formed resulted from expansion within, or movement from, pre-existing communities.

Whether they came from existing communities or were new immigrants, Amish settlers moved west along established routes. Here again, the Somerset County settlements played a crucial role in Amish migration, not only by spawning daughter colonies but also in providing staging posts for migrating families. Located just south of the Huntingdon, Cambria, and Indiana Turnpike (built c.1810), and close by the railroads that were later laid down near Johnstown—linking west-central Pennsylvania to Philadelphia and the East Coast—the Conemaugh congregation was just one of the Somerset/Cambria communities that facilitated the onward migration of their Amish brethren. But increasingly, as the nineteenth century progressed, new immigrants from Europe by-passed the pioneer trail routes that connected the old-established Amish communities and found river and canal-based routes from the north and south into the Midwest.[12]

Amish Society in Nineteenth-century America

As the nineteenth century began, the Amish in America numbered barely 1,000-1,200 individuals. By the turn of the twentieth century their numbers had increased significantly, and they had spread westwards, southwards and northwards, farming land in at least fifteen U.S. states, together with Ontario in Canada. However, many of the nineteenth-century Amish communities were transient ones, some lasting as little as twenty years. Others survived longer but died out as adverse circumstances, including growing industrialization, rising land costs, and declining soil fertility, pressured communities to move ever onward in order to maintain their rural way of life.

Communities also fragmented as the result of schisms within the Amish church. No account of any aspect of Amish society in nineteenth-century America can ignore the impact of the profound disagreements that eventually fractured the Amish church in the 1860s. The roots of these divisions had begun before mid-century, for as the Amish community grew in numbers it became harder to retain cohesion and to coordinate a response to America's increasing prosperity and consumerism. Amish society polarized into what has been described as a 'change-minded' group and a 'tradition-minded' group.[13] Whether specific communities were change-minded or tradition-minded was often a reflection of the roots of that community; those with Ohio roots tended to be more progressive than those from Pennsylvania. As Crowley has shown, the newer immigrants from Europe were also less conservative, creating further tensions within the longer-established communities—in Pennsylvania, in particular.

By the late 1840s, progressive (i.e. change-minded) Amish leaders were favoring a more inclusive approach to Amish society within America and exhibited a greater desire to fit into their new country's ways. This was an attitude that could be given visible expression through more fashionable clothing and household furnishings, formal education, and taking advantage of opportunities to hold public office. To the more tradition-minded, this was not an acceptable route; they considered it undermining their faith values of simplicity, humility, and communal decision-making. In the event, these divisions could not be reconciled, and two decades later the Amish church divided. One-third of the former Amish community formed the traditionalist Old Order Amish, whilst the majority grouping became Amish Mennonites. Nevertheless, further internal differences remained within each of these two groups, with each eventually sub-dividing further as individual communities found separate ways to confront the challenges of social change. For the traditional Amish group, the group within which classic Amish quilts were made, new communities were formed that were either more liberal or more conservative than those at the core. Gradually, each community developed distinct visual codes for transport and dress—codes that signalled their community identity. And as a result of this process, they could be visually separated not only from mainstream society but also from each other, and it is these visual symbols—different hats, braces, bonnets, and buggy tops, for example—that are familiar markers in Amish society today.

It appears, however, that such (now commonplace) visual markers were not always found within nineteenth-century Amish society itself. Before the 1860s schisms, the evidence suggests that the Amish in America appeared little different from the non-Amish: neither in dress, lifestyle, nor in farming practice. In recording this lack of distinctiveness in the first half of the nineteenth century, Steven Nolt set Amish dress in the context of the larger Germanic group of which the Amish were a part:

> [Amish] wills and estate inventories do not suggest a notable presence or absence of particular household goods or equipment ... English colonists often remarked on the peculiar dress of Pennsylvania Germans ... Undoubtedly the Amish demonstrated a commitment to simplicity in appearance, but the form that such plainness took may have been somewhat less striking in their ethnic context.[14]

In his account of why the contemporary Amish dress as they do, Stephen Scott also related Amish dress to that of other peasant communities: "Several scholars theorized that plain dress is an adaptation of styles that were once fashionable or a carry-over from peasant clothing."[15] So whilst Amish dress might have become a coda of identity in the twentieth century, in the nineteenth century it appears to have differed little from the dress of immigrant farming families from other European backgrounds, including Welsh and British immigrants from both industrial and rural Britain. Theron Schlabach concurred with this lack of distinction between the Amish and non-Amish as it existed before the 1860s, highlighting the level of mixing and interaction between the two:

> ...in daily life Mennonites and Amish constantly mixed with their neighbors in mills, distilleries, markets and shops. Even attire and pacifism did not draw formidable lines ... there is not much

evidence that clothing caused early-nineteenth-century Mennonites and Amish to stand out sharply.[16]

Though the evidence is sparse, there seems every reason to conclude that there was no outward distinction between conjunct Amish and non-Amish groups in the period before the 1860s. Moreover, there appears to have been a greater degree of interaction between them than existed a century later, particularly amongst the more liberal Amish wing with its aspirations to participate in public life. It was largely after the 1860s schisms that those in the conservative Old Order Amish were discouraged from adopting the manifestations of consumerism that subsequently distanced them from mainstream society. There are indications of this in a letter from one Amish bishop to another, in 1882, in which the writer emphasizes how much he regrets "unnecessary clothing finery."[17] It was also in the post-division 1860s that the tradition-minded Amish were encouraged to: "separate themselves from worldly carnivals, the pride and wasted expense of 'speckled, striped, flowered, clothing' and from 'unnecessary grand, household furnishings'."[18] It was within this backdrop of change and discontent in the nineteenth-century Amish community, but apparently in a climate of closer interaction between Amish and non-Amish until the divisions, that Amish women adopted what had become a widespread practice amongst non-Amish women: the making of quilts.

Amish Quilt-making: Early Developments in Time and Place

Limitations of evidence make it difficult for quilt historians to reach a firm view as to the precise period when Amish quilt-making began, but the consensus is that it did not begin before the mid-1800s. There is also a view that Amish quilt-making began in Pennsylvania and spread, geographically, to

3.7. Block wool quilt, Single Irish Chain, Amish, hand sewn, Elkhart County Indiana, 1840–1850, 85" x 86" (216 cm x 218 cm). *From the Collection of the Indiana State Museum and Historic Sites.*

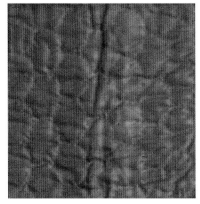

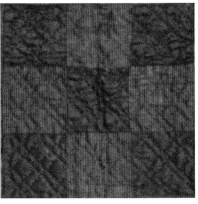

3.8. Detail of Nine Patch pieced wool quilt,
Amish; for full quilt see Figure 3.13.
From the Collection of the Indiana State Museum and Historic Sites.

3.9. Block quilt, Feathered Star, Amish, c. 1850–1870,
66" x 79" (167 cm x 200 cm).
Courtesy of the International Quilt Study Center & Museum,
University of Nebraska–Lincoln, 1997.007.0161.

3.10. Detail of block quilt, Crosses and Losses, Amish; for full quilt *see* Figure 1.10. *From the Collection of the Indiana State Museum and Historic Sites.*

3.11. Wholecloth quilt in glazed cotton, Amish, initialled 'G. D.' and dated '1869', possibly made in Pennsylvania, 87" x 87" (221 cm x 221 cm). *From the Collection of the Indiana State Museum and Historic Sites.*

other states as a result of the general Amish migration westward. Significantly though, the affirmed Amish settlement histories appear to conflict with this theoretical standpoint of migration transfer, for by the mid-1800s (when Amish quilt-making is supposed to have only just begun) many Amish settlers had already moved well beyond Pennsylvania itself and on into the Midwest. Indeed, Amish migration into the Midwest had begun as early as c.1808, though conversely the earliest surviving Amish quilts come from no earlier than late in the 1840s, and few examples are dated to before 1870. Of the handful of Amish quilts believed to pre-date 1875, those from the Midwest shown in Figures 3.4, 3.5, 3.7 and 3.8 are all block designs. Most are hand-sewn in wools with unsophisticated pieced designs but two exceptions are a Feathered Star quilt from Ohio (Figure 3.9) and a Bow Tie/Crosses and Losses quilt from Indiana (Figure 3.10). The sole surviving examples with apparent Pennsylvanian provenances, two Wholecloth cotton quilts, are carefully stitched with well-planned quilting designs and both bear initialed and dated inscriptions: '1849' and '1869' respectively. One is illustrated in Figure 3.11, but the other documented example could not be traced.[19] Considered overall, there is no common character within these (pre-1870) quilts beyond the use of plain cloth, nor is there any obvious progression in style. The Midwest wool quilts appear more homely and more coarsely stitched; indeed, one was used as the filling to a later 'comforter,' a use which signifies its lack of value as a decorative bed covering but emphasizes its practical value for warmth.

From the written record, wills and estate inventories confirm that Amish families owned quilts from the 1830s onwards, though inventories that list 'quilts' amongst an Amish household's stock of bedding are rare until the 1870s–1880s. Despite the paucity of quilt listings in Amish estate papers between 1830 and 1870, Grannick's extensive work on such documents from Pennsylvania and the Midwest noted that, both in Ohio and in Pennsylvania, quilts first appear in estate records in the 1830s and, significantly, they actually appear earlier and more often in Ohio (to the west) than in Pennsylvania:

... a substantial number of quilts are included in Amish estate records [in Ohio]. One of the most noteworthy aspects of these listings is the early dates at which quilts appear in the Ohio communities and the relatively large number that are listed ... The earliest notation of quilts in Pennsylvanian Amish inventories is in Mifflin County in 1836 ... In Ohio, the first listing of quilts appeared in 1831 ... Though quilts do not appear in Amish estate papers with the same frequency as they appear in the inventories of non-German families in Ohio, they do appear more frequently than in Pennsylvanian Amish documents.[20]

In considering Grannick's evidence, Holstein reached the conclusion that "it is not certain whether Amish quilts were made first by the Amish of Pennsylvania or the Midwest."[21] Correlating the time-lines and stylistic differences in surviving quilts that are believed to date from before 1870 certainly raises doubts about the location (or locations) where Amish quilt-making first began. Given the differences in Amish quilt style between the Lancaster tradition and the Midwest tradition, then it could be that Amish quilt-making had no single seminal source, but emerged differentially from parallel strands in time and place. Those strands could include the increasing availability of inexpensive, factory-produced fabrics from the 1830s onwards. In a recent study of historic inventories in Lancaster County, Pennsylvania, it was concluded that this factor was significant in the adoption of quilt-making amongst all Pennsylvanian Germans, including the Amish, in the mid-nineteenth century.[22]

The evidence contained in estate records is vital in building up a picture of the early use and production of Amish quilts but, regrettably, few such records contain physical descriptions of the quilts recorded. Of the hundreds of inventories studied by Grannick, the only descriptive phrase discovered was in an 1849 inventory from Mifflin County, referring to an "old woolen brown quilt."[23] A little additional detail comes from a ledger compiled by one of the original founders of the Moultrie/Douglas Old Order Amish community in Illinois, the community that originated from Somerset County, Pennsylvania. Daniel D. Otto listed the items he wished to pass on to his children. In his 1881 entries he bequeathed: "two quilts" and "1 Flannel quilt" to a daughter; and "1 calico quilt" and two "flannel quilts" to a son.[24] These entries suggest a recognized distinction between flannel (i.e. wool) quilts and other quilts, e.g. the calico quilt, though the implications of this remain speculative. The use of the appellation "flannel" amongst the Old Order Amish is of particular note in this context; it is the common Welsh term for wool cloth.

Though they remain some of the 'hardest' evidence available, the quilts listed in wills and inventories need to be considered in a temporal context; they may well have been made some time before the date of the written record. The question of terminology also has to be considered. What is meant by a 'quilt' in the context of these nineteenth-century inventories? In studying Amish inventories from the 1830s–1870s, Grannick reported a very low rate of 'quilt' ownership but she also records that: "Haps, coverlets, comforts, blankets and chaff beds appear to have been the dominant form of bed covering, rather than quilts."[25] But how did the nineteenth-century compilers of these inventories distinguish 'comforts,' 'coverlets,' and 'haps' from 'quilts?' It cannot be assumed that their categorizations equate to the common use of the same terms today. In her oral-history research in central Pennsylvania in the 1970s and 1980s, Jeanette Lasansky observed:

> Consistently [quilt-makers] called heavy bed coverings, either knotted or quilted, "comforts," "comfortables," or "haps" and the words were interchangeable. A hap was always thick and heavy. They were often, although not always, filled with wool (sometimes cotton or a worn quilt) and usually knotted. Those that were quilted were done with coarser though even quilting, usually five stitches to the inch.[26]

Lasansky's definition of a 'hap,' when quilted rather than tied, is uncannily like a definition of a Welsh wool quilt, right down to the five stitches per inch, and indeed the word is of British (though not Welsh) origin. It was in common use in Northern England and Scotland in the nineteenth and early twentieth centuries as a dialect term for a warm

wool quilt, generally of a more utilitarian than refined character. In that same sense, it survived in central and parts of southern Pennsylvania amongst the Welsh and Pennsylvanian Germans. And 'hap' is also a term that occurs in the Amish inventories from Mifflin County, though not apparently elsewhere.[27] What is intriguing is that this vernacular term—used by the immigrant group that David Hackett Fischer inclusively called the "North British"[28]—apparently crossed over into the lexicon of other ethnic groups in Pennsylvania, keeping the same specific meaning that it had in Britain, i.e. a thick warm bedcover. More strikingly still, Pennsylvanian usage of the word 'hap' survived well into the late twentieth century.

Interestingly, Lasansky recorded one bedcover from central Pennsylvania, known in the family concerned as a 'hap,' that would be categorized today as a 'quilt.' It is illustrated in Figure 3.12. Comparing this hap/quilt to the Amish quilt in Figure 3.4, itself used as the inside of a 'comfort,' and to the quilts in Figures 3.13 and 3.14, it seems possible that early Amish wool quilts like these might have been recorded in inventories not as quilts but alternatively as haps, comforts or comforters, terms which Grannick records as figuring much more prominently than 'quilt' in Amish inventories between 1830 and the 1870s.[29]

In conclusion, and to return to the main focus of this book, if the presence of nineteenth-century Welsh immigrants did influence early developments in Amish quilt-making, then the likelihood is that these nineteenth-century immigrants would have been located—as visible communities—in the vicinity of permanent or transient Amish settlements. In the next chapter, research findings will be presented that identify and describe just such nineteenth-century locations where Welsh immigrants established locally-significant settlements in close proximity to Amish communities. Then, in Chapter 5, select community conjunctions of this kind will be further highlighted in order to underscore places where, on the basis of previously little-explored evidence, it is entirely plausible that Welsh and Amish social interactions probably took place and relevant cultural cross-overs may have occurred.

3.12. Huber family 'hap', nineteenth-century bedcovering filled with wool and quilted with 5-6 stitches per inch, East Buffalo Township, Union County Pennsylvania, 60" x 72" (152 cm x 183 cm).
Courtesy of 'In the Heart of Pennsylvania': Oral Traditions Project of the Union County Historical Society.

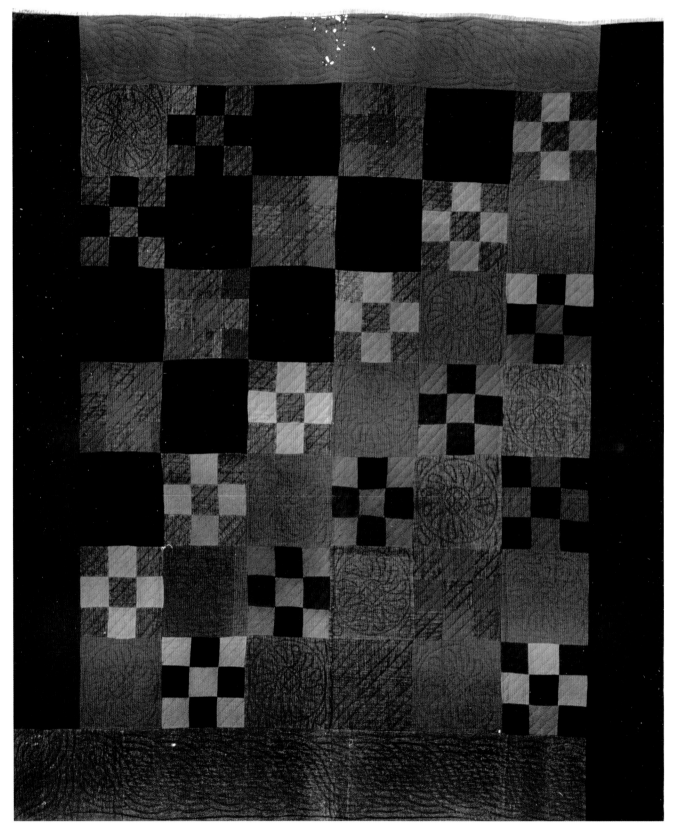

3.13. Block wool quilt, Nine Patch, Amish, Lagrange County Indiana,
thickly padded and quilted with five stitches per inch, 1880-1900, 70" x 80" (178 cm x 203 cm).
From the Collection of the Indiana State Museum and Historic Sites.

3.14. Scrap quilt, Amish, pieced in wools
by Magdalena Fisher Yoder of Illinois,
c. 1875, 63" x 74" (160 cm x 188 cm).
Courtesy of Illinois State Museum.

4

Welsh Emigration and Settlement in Nineteenth-century America

> If I had come to this country four to six years sooner, I would not have needed to take off my hat to any man. If I have my life and health for a little while I shall be a burden to no one. ... Whoever has the heart and the resolution to come here will never be sorry after he once sets foot on the land ... This country differs greatly from Wales ... I live better here now than I have ever lived before.
>
> (David Jones: letter from Albany, NY,
> to his wife in Wales, 14 October 1817)[1]

*I*T WAS IN SUCH LETTERS OF PRAISE for their new country to families back home that prospering settlers gave encouragement to the wave of Welsh emigrants that crossed the Atlantic for a new home in America in the nineteenth century. Unlike their predecessors in the previous two centuries, most of this group of later (i.e. nineteenth-century) Welsh emigrants were not primarily seeking religious freedom. They were economic migrants seeking to escape the control of landlords and government taxation, and seeking to acquire the social freedoms denied by the hierarchical structure of Britain's class-ridden society. It was these nineteenth-century Welsh emigrants, not those from previous centuries, who seem likely to have brought with them the quilts that bear comparison with Amish quilts.

Of course, not all emigrants prospered as did David Jones. But the majority of those who crossed the Atlantic between the 1790s (when this particular migration wave began) and 1900 remained in their new homeland, establishing successful lives for themselves and their families. And it was the picture they painted in their homeward-bound correspondence—that of a 'promised land'—that became the biggest 'pull' factor in many a nineteenth-century emigrant's decision to leave their native homeland.[2] It was a 'pull' to the New World that was also facilitated by a network of employers' agents, based in Wales, who gave encouragement, both in cash and in kind, to prospective emigrant workers.

In the first half of the nineteenth century, Welsh emigration to America had a mixed rural–industrial character. The goal of many Welsh emigrants was simply to acquire land, even if they had to take on initial labouring or industrial jobs to acquire sufficient capital to do so. Initially, with good prospective farmland, the states of New York, Pennsylvania, and Ohio were particular magnets. For Pennsylvania, the wave of nineteenth-century Welsh immigration was just the latest phase in a connection that had been on-going for well over a hundred years. Welsh settlers to Pennsylvania were, in fact, part of the main Quaker settlement of Philadelphia and its hinterland in the 1680s. Indeed, Welsh Quakers had grouped together and settled on fertile lands purchased from William Penn to the north and west of Philadelphia in 1682. Like other Quakers, they came to America seeking religious freedom and established what became known as the 'Welsh Tract.' So enthusiastic did these Welsh Quakers and a later group of Welsh Baptists become about Penn's new colony that, by the beginning of the eighteenth century, they accounted for a third of the population of 20,000.[3]

From the beginning, colonial Welsh immigrants played an integral part in the life of their new province; within a generation they had ceased to be Welsh-speaking and had lost their ethnic identity. Leaders amongst the Welsh community, who were described as "men of substance but not of great wealth,"[4] came to form an élite in the Welsh Tract area west of the Schuylkill River. Later to become a nineteenth-century settler himself, the Welsh Congregational minister, the Reverend R.D. Thomas, provided a flavour of this immigrant group (as he saw them) during an earlier exploratory visit in 1851–52:

Many Welsh people from Montgomeryshire [Mid-Wales] and Merioneth [North Wales] came to Philadelphia over two hundred years ago. Some preceded the famous William Penn, the Quakers accompanied him, others followed... The descendants of the Welshmen are the majority of the population of "Dyffryn Mawr" or the Counties of Montgomery? [sic] and Chester near Philadelphia. But most of them have lost their mother tongue. ...They are mostly wealthy people, many of them honest tradespeople, some physicians, councilors and judges etc and have a respect for their country.[5]

From the Welsh Tract area of Delaware, Chester, and Montgomery counties, Welsh settlers gradually spread out into Bucks and Berks counties. By 1700 there was also a small group of Welsh settlers in Lancaster County, and by 1750 they had moved in along the Susquehanna frontier.[6] But the overall proportion and standing of the Welsh in eighteenth-century Pennsylvania dwindled as a result of increased immigration by other groups, for instance, the Germans and 'Scotch–Irish.' The pioneering legacy of this first wave of Welsh immigration to Pennsylvania survives today in township names such as: Lampeter in Lancaster County; Caernarvon and Brecknock in both Lancaster and Berks counties; Cumru (after *Cymru*, the Welsh word for Wales) in Berks County; and Nantmeal, Tredyffrin and Uwchlan in Chester County. It also persists in designations such as the 'Welsh Mountain'—the upland area that straddles Chester and Lancaster counties—though this eighteenth-century place-name came to acquire a negative image when nineteenth-century lawlessness from the non-Welsh 'Buzzard Gang' gave that mountain area (and the Welsh by association) a dubious reputation.[7]

Census records, however, indicate little evidence of continuing Welsh immigration into this original diaspora from relatives and communities back home. Though descendants of the pre-1800 Welsh migrants spread out widely in Pennsylvania and, in the early nineteenth century, were close to the early Amish settlers of Lancaster County's Conestoga Valley, their Welsh identity had been lost and ties to their homeland had long since ceased to be close. Interestingly, it was members of this 'Welsh' group who were documented as having sold land to the Amish when they left Berks County for the Conestoga valley (see Chapter 3), but the likelihood that they had any influence in the development of quilt-making amongst the Amish is considered remote. Although emigrants from seventeenth- and eighteenth-century Britain would likely have brought household possessions with them, they were largely migrants from the higher echelons of British society and their domestic textiles would have reflected that status. If they brought quilts with them, they were unlikely to have been wool quilts, the vernacular quilt genre that has been shown (see Chapter 6) to have close connection to early and classic Amish quilts. And if they made quilts in America, the rapid absorption of this group into American society suggests that their cultural influences did not remain closely linked to their Celtic background.

Nineteenth-century Welsh Immigration: Implications for Cultural Cross-over

It is the later Welsh immigrations that have potential relevance to an Amish–Welsh quilt-making connection. Beginning in the 1790s, and extending through the growing industrialization of America, the great wave of nineteenth-century Welsh immigration began with rural migrants settling in New York State, Pennsylvania, and Ohio. For Pennsylvania, the first significant new Welsh settlement was founded in 1796 in what was then Somerset County, with the establishment of a Welsh farming community in the west-central part of the state which grew into the town of Ebensburg. In his classic Welsh text *The Welsh in America*, published in 1872, the Rev. R.D. Thomas gave a graphic account of Ebensburg, Cambria County, the new county created in 1804 and named by its Welsh settlers after their homeland:

This place is located in the Allegheny mountains. The settlement was begun by the Rev. Morgan J. Rees, a Baptist, and the Rev. George Roberts, a Congregationalist, about the year 1796. They began to work on the land near Beulah, and later decided to build the

town on the small hill where it is now located… The majority of the inhabitants are Welsh, and several of them are men of riches, learning, and influence. Welsh farmers have bought the land for miles around the town and live comfortably on it… the Baptists, the Calvinist Methodists and the Congregationalists still have Welsh churches there.[8]

The Welsh enclave established in Cambria County in the early nineteenth century not only attracted new Welsh settlers but also became a springboard for the westward movement of other Welsh migrants. At the same time and just a few miles to the south, Amish communities in Somerset County were functioning in just the same way: as a fulcrum of movement from central and eastern Pennsylvanian into the Midwest states. From Cambria County, Welsh immigrants moved into western Ohio as early as 1801 and founded a sizeable Welsh settlement there—in Butler County, Southwest Ohio. By 1850, new Welsh settlements had also been established in seven other counties across Central, Southeast, Northeast, and Northwest Ohio (see the map in Figure 4.1). As rural farming settlements, they continued to attract Welsh farmers and their families throughout the nineteenth century, some of whom had simply moved on from Pennsylvania, but others were new transatlantic immigrants direct from Wales. Three of the Ohio counties settled by the Welsh before 1850 also contained Amish pioneer settlements, whilst others were contiguous with, or little distant from, counties with Amish communities.

Like the Amish and other ethnic groups, some Welsh settlers moved on as lands further west, in Indiana and Illinois, were opened up. After 1840 they progressed, most significantly to Wisconsin, but also to Iowa, Minnesota and beyond. These westward migrants were seeking land but, even as they moved west, the character of Welsh immigration changed for America's growing prosperity was now creating a demand for skilled industrial labour. With expertise honed in the coal, iron and steel industries of South Wales, many Welsh immigrants were well-placed to take advantage of this demand, and came

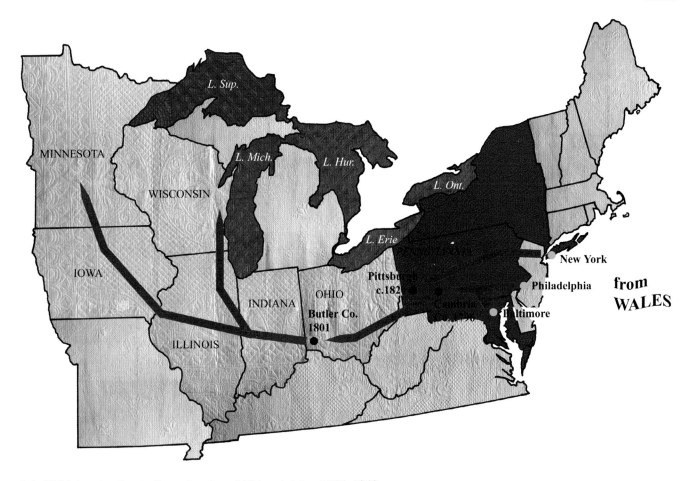

4.1. Welsh immigration to Pennsylvania and Midwest states: 1796–1860.

to make a contribution to America's developing economy over and above their numbers. In the words of American academic, William Van Vugt:

> The American coal industry owes a lot to the modest numbers of Welsh immigrants who settled in the United States during the nineteenth century. More than any other group, they unlocked America's vast coal reserves with the advanced skills and methods that they had acquired in the mother country. The Welsh were also important for the development of related industries, especially iron. In both the coal and iron industries the Welsh prospered and rose to become mine bosses, operators and owners.[9]

Beginning in the 1820s, Pittsburgh became the focal point for the first industrial Welsh immigrants; they were followed by a regular flow of Welsh migrants into western Pennsylvania through much of the nineteenth century. They came to work in Pittsburgh's iron and steel industries and, by the second half of the nineteenth century, Welsh immigrants made up around a fifth of the city's population.[10] When rich mineral reserves were found in Cambria County, Pennsylvania, already the location of a significant Welsh diaspora, the area became another mecca for Welsh workers as the coal and iron industries established around Ebensburg and Johnstown expanded, and demand for industrial skills increased. The 1850 census records show that almost three-quarters of the foreign-born population in the area around Ebensburg were Welsh-born.[11]

Though both industrial and rural Welsh immigrants spread throughout the U.S. as nineteenth-century America grew and prospered, Pennsylvania still exercised a magnetic 'pull' for the Welsh. The attraction lay not just in its historic association with Wales but in the employment opportunities offered when the full extent of the rich reserves of Pennsylvania's coal and slate

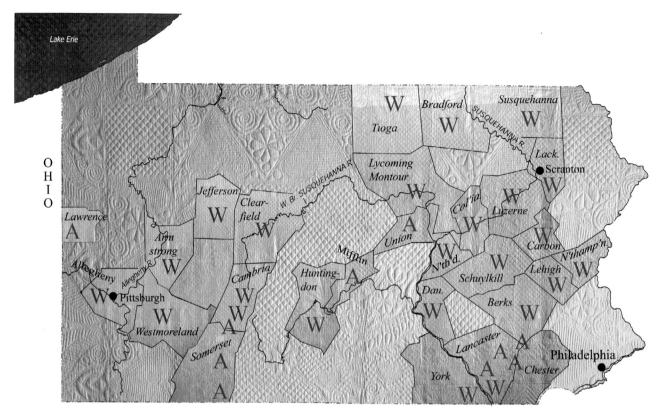

4.2. Pennsylvania counties which had nineteenth-century Welsh settlements adjacent to nineteenth-century Amish settlements. *Key to abbreviations:* W = counties with Welsh settlements, A = counties with Amish settlements;

Col'ia = Columbia Co., Dau = Dauphin Co., N'thamp'n = Northampton Co., N'th'd = Northumberland Co. *Data sources:* Thomas, 1872; and Jones, W. D., 1993.

belts became known. With the opening of the anthracite coal belt of northeastern Pennsylvania, Welsh workers flooded in, establishing large Welsh communities in and around Scranton and Wilkes-Barre. In his book *Wales in America: Scranton and the Welsh, 1860–1920*, William D. Jones commented that: "the singular feature of Welsh settlement in the United States during [the 1880–1900 period] is the remarkable concentration of the Welsh in one state, Pennsylvania. Here, in 1900, lived nearly 38% of the 93,586 first-generation Welsh in the United States."[12]

Located in and around the industrial centres of the northeast of the state, and around Pittsburgh in the west, these large Welsh diasporas of nineteenth-century Pennsylvania were not located particularly close to Pennsylvania's Amish communities. It seems unlikely that Welsh communities in the northeastern region of Pennsylvania would have had much opportunity for contact with nineteenth-century Amish communities, which were all located

in the southern, central and western areas of the state. But Welsh industrial immigrants settled along the length of the extensive Pennsylvanian coal belt and, in 1872, Thomas identified notable Welsh communities in eighteen separate Pennsylvanian counties, all of which are shown on the map in Figure 4.2.[13] Of these smaller communities, the Cambria County groups around Ebensburg and Johnstown are of particular interest. Not only did they originate as farming settlements, but they were close to the Amish 'Conemaugh' settlement of Somerset County and, similarly, were located on westward migration routes.

If coalmining and ironworking attracted contemporary observers' greatest attention, then nineteenth-century America also had need of another long established Welsh industrial skill: slate quarrying. The reserves of Pennsylvania's slate belt had been known since the eighteenth century, but as industrial and urban expansion gained pace, slate quarries opened up in southeastern

4.3. The Bethesda Welsh Congregational Church built in West Bangor, York County Pennsylvania in 1857; the church and church community were photographed in 1885. *Courtesy of Old Line Museum, Delta.*

Pennsylvania—in York and Lancaster counties—in the 1840s, and further north in Northampton County, around the town of Bangor, so-named after its counterpart in North Wales. Though this new Bangor became the centre of the Pennsylvanian slate industry, it is the Welsh quarrying communities established in York and Lancaster counties in the 1840s that have greater significance in relation to a possible Amish–Welsh quilt-making connection. Located on either side of the Susquehanna River, a transport and communications artery of mid-nineteenth-century, south-eastern Pennsylvania, these quarry-based settlements were within a few miles of the Lancaster County Amish.

Unlike their seventeenth- and eighteenth-century counterparts, nineteenth-century Welsh immigrants did retain a strong cultural identity, settling in ethnic enclaves and retaining their original language and customs. Though they had not left Wales fleeing religious persecution, they were still deeply religious, so an early priority was to establish chapels, churches, and Sunday schools (Figure 4.3). Overwhelmingly nonconformist and anti-slavery, their faith and community connections were maintained by travelling ministers in much the same way as in Amish communities. In this way, the Welsh in rural communities experienced a religious continuity that the English and Scots did not always have.

From a twenty-first century perspective the Welsh may now be considered one of America's 'invisible immigrant' groups, but there seems little doubt that nineteenth-century Welsh enclaves maintained their cultural visibility for some length of time. Written in the first decade of the 1900s, one account of the Welsh Hills settlement in Licking County, Ohio, records that: "The population has preserved its character as a distinctly Welsh settlement until very recent years."[14] It has to be recognized however, that the contribution of the Welsh to the overall population growth of nineteenth-century America was quantitatively very small, even if they did, as Van Vugt has argued, punch qualitatively above their weight in progressing U.S. industrialization. And despite the fact that Welsh immigration was almost certainly underestimated in official statistics—the Welsh were persistently classified as 'English'—they still represent a comparatively small ethnic group. At the peak in 1891, the U.S. census recorded around 100,000 Welsh-born residents out of a total population of around 75 million. With a population in Wales of only around a million in the middle of the nineteenth century and with a much smaller proportion of emigrants than Ireland (a country of similar population size), the history of nineteenth-century Welsh settlement in America has largely been eclipsed by that of bigger national groups such as the Germans, Irish, and English (with which they were statistically linked). Of the total number of immigrants from England and Wales between 1820 and 1900, it is estimated that only 2.5% were Welsh,[15] though figures extracted from ships' passenger lists for 1820–1845 suggest that, of the approximately 650,000 'English and Welsh' immigrants recorded, the proportion of Welsh was then distinctly higher: approximately 6%.[16]

However small the proportion of nineteenth-century American immigrants from Wales might have been, surviving evidence emphasizes the significance of Pennsylvania and Ohio as their destinations of choice: the same states first settled by the Amish. Should further emphasis be needed, the figures given in the 1900 census for Welsh-born immigrants show that Pennsylvania alone held over a third of the Welsh diaspora in America in 1900, with Ohio holding the next largest population of Welsh origin. After that, only New York, Illinois, and Wisconsin had populations of Welsh-born individuals totalling more than 3,000. Furthermore, if Welsh immigration was relatively small in scale compared to the level of U.S. immigration as a whole, in 1900 the total population in Welsh settlements still significantly outnumbered the 5,000 persons estimated to represent their immigrant counterparts: the Old Order Amish.

Admittedly, many of these nineteenth-century Welsh immigrants lived in industrial areas remote from the Amish farming communities of Ohio and Pennsylvania, but the study outlined above has clearly identified two areas of Pennsylvania where Welsh and Amish communities were in sufficiently close proximity for social interaction to be a real possibility: Cambria County in west-central Pennsylvania, adjacent to and originally part of Somerset County; and Lancaster and York counties in southeastern Pennsylvania, adjacent to and across the river from the Lancaster County Amish. These two geographic conjunctions hold particular import since they existed at a point in time when Amish quilt-making is believed to have begun in the U.S. The study has also identified specific regions in Ohio where Welsh communities lay close to active nineteenth-century Amish communities. This potential Ohio connection has hitherto been obscured by the fact that—despite the large and thriving Amish community still centred on Holmes County today—some of these places did not survive (as Old Order Amish settlements) beyond the late nineteenth century.

The next chapter (Chapter 5) will focus on these Pennsylvania and Ohio settlements. But prior to that it is pertinent to examine how nineteenth-century Welsh emigrants arrived in the U.S. and, most importantly for the quilt narrative, to make reasoned attempt to gauge the kinds of domestic goods that they brought with them.

The Emigrant Experience

Whether eager for adventure or wary of leaving home, or both, there was no shortage of advice and encouragement on hand for the many would-be Welsh emigrants to America in

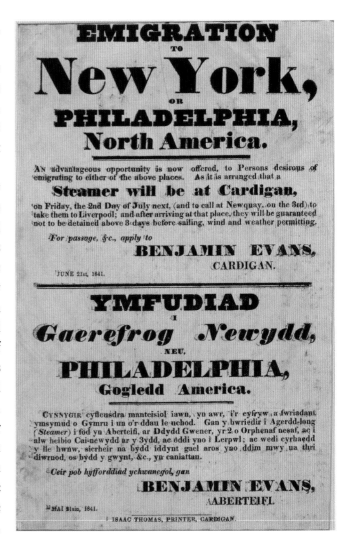

4.4. Poster advertising passage from Cardigan and Newquay, South West Wales, on a steamer to Liverpool then transfer to an emigration ship to New York or Philadelphia, 1841. *By permission of Llyfrgell Genedlaethol Cymru/The National Library of Wales (Wales–Pennsylvania Project).*

the nineteenth century. Letters from family and friends already settled across the Atlantic were a major encouragement, not only on the prospects for land or work that awaited the emigrant but also on the sea-passage, the perils of which are too often exaggerated today. Though death and disease were not uncommon, and shipwreck was undoubtedly an *ever-present* danger, the biggest problem most emigrants faced on board ship was sea-sickness, that is until (and if) they got their sea-legs. The majority arrived in good health and comparatively good spirits. In company with other Welsh emigrants, young William Griffiths sailed for America during the spring of 1836 and described the experience in a letter to his parents back in Wales:

As well as encouragement from those who had blazed the transatlantic trail, a variety of publications gave advice and information to the would-be emigrant, advice that was commonly available in other European countries as well. Geared to the prospective Welsh settler in Pennsylvania, *Instructions for the Immigrant* (1866) gave more detailed information than most, describing where the Welsh already were, in what numbers, and what religious and social benefits a newcomer might anticipate. The booklet further detailed the wages that could be expected in particular industries, and gave instructions on how to travel to specific locations upon arrival. For emigrant quarrymen going to the slate quarries of York County, Pennsylvania, the advice was to:

> ...take a train from Philadelphia to Oxford and a carriage from there to Peter's Creek [Lancaster County], on the banks of the Susquehanna; then in a boat over the river to West Bangor and Slate Hill ... It is only 49 miles from Philadelphia to Oxford, and one can get from there to Peter's Creek in a few hours. Slate quarries are the main characteristic of these settlements, and people from North Wales are living there primarily. They are good places for quarrymen, and there are many Welsh who have succeeded notably there. The village is located in York county on rocky hill land which is healthful and pleasant. There are all religious advantages, good Welsh chapels, etc. [18]

It was through formal communication channels such as this, together with the informal encouragement of kith and kin, that chain migration and cultural continuity was maintained in nineteenth-century Welsh enclaves in America.

In the early years of the nineteenth century, some emigrants from South Wales sailed from Bristol or on ships from one of the smaller ports around the coast of South and South West Wales. From North Wales, too, the pre-1850 emigrant might find passage on a small ship from a local port such as Aberystwyth or Cardigan, or perhaps on a slate-carrying schooner bound direct for America,

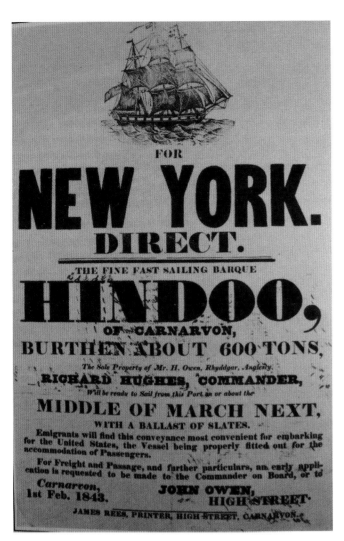

4.5. Poster advertising passage on the slate-carrying sailing barque *Hindoo* from Caernarfon, North Wales, 1843. *Courtesy of Gwynedd Record Office.*

We took ship in Liverpool in a vessel called the Constitution ... and had a good wind for two or three days ... I was rather ill the first week but mercifully I soon got better. Within about a fortnight it began to blow strongly and it lasted for twenty-four hours. We met a ship from London and sailed together for eight or nine days. They offered us a doctor but we were all quite well and happy ... After being five weeks without seeing land we saw America for the first time ... We had to stay twenty-four hours in quarantine while the officials and doctors came to examine us. I paid £4 for the journey from Liverpool to Baltimore and 30s. for food and everything from Baltimore to Pittsburgh. I went there on foot except for twenty-eight miles.[17]

4.6. Canning Dock in the emigration port of Liverpool, 1830s.

as evidenced by the sailing poster in Figure 4.5. But by the time *Instructions for the Immigrant* was published (1866), most Welsh emigrants left from the English port of Liverpool, close to the English–Welsh border, for by the second half of the nineteenth century the burgeoning port of Liverpool had captured the greater part of Welsh emigrant traffic. (For the location of Liverpool, see the map of Wales and its environs in Figure 2.5.) Until the early 1860s, most of these emigrants crossed in regularly-scheduled sailing ships known as 'packets,' but by 1870 steamships had replaced these sailing vessels, cutting travelling time and passage costs as well.

Whatever the exact modes of sea transport, or wherever the departure was from, it is appropriate in the context of this study to question whether or not these Welsh emigrants took quilts and their vernacular quilt-making knowledge with them. In the wealth of historical documentation that details emigrant profiles, origins, and passages made, there is no immediate evidence that describes quilts as part of the possessions that accompanied either single emigrants or family groups. Conversely, there is good indirect evidence to confirm that, if emigrants took little else with them, they would have taken their own clothes and bedding. Like other passengers on the transatlantic voyage, most Welsh emigrants travelled steerage, the cheapest form of accommodation, and were advised to provide various shipboard essentials, always including personal bedding. In steerage accommodation, emigrants lived in "temporary communal dormitories, each family allocated a bunk, or perhaps two if there were more than two children. These temporary bunks built in space normally occupied by cargo, were generally in two

4.7. Typical sleeping accommodation for steerage passengers on mid-nineteenth-century emigrant ships.

tiers, one above the other. Sanitation consisted of buckets, sometimes fitted with seats. There were no special washing places."[19] If the passage to America was less hazardous than popularly assumed, for steerage passengers it was undoubtedly cramped and smelly.

From 1842 onwards, the British Passenger Acts increasingly sought to regulate emigrant transport conditions, ensuring minimum levels of provisioning—but little more. So, although emigrants were fed and watered, steerage passengers were still issued with instructions to provide "… their own Utensils and Bedding. The Articles required are Beds, Bedding, Towels, Knife and Fork…"[20] In what was popularly known as *Murray's Guide for Emigrants* (1843), the author sternly emphasized the need to take bed covers: "The only articles which it is expedient to take out, beyond those

required upon the voyage, are bedding and a good stock of substantial clothing. Emigrants should not neglect this, or they will sincerely regret it." Once in America, emigrants moving inland via canal or river were yet again required to "have their bedding, provisions and cooking utensils on board."[21] An even earlier more individual exhortation to bring bedding was contained in a letter from Warren County, New York, in 1817 in which John Richards advised: "Those who come over should bring as many clothes as they can and bedclothes because they are very dear here."[22]

So taking bedding was vital, not only for the passage itself but also for life and thrift in the New World. Given the widespread use of quilts as bedcovers in nineteenth-century Wales, and the character of the emigration movements from rural and industrial Wales described above, it is

4.8. Typical eating accommodation for steerage passengers on mid-nineteenth-century emigrant ships.

reasonable to conclude that weighty, warm Welsh wool quilts—the quilts with most visual connection to Amish quilts—did accompany emigrants across the Atlantic. Are any known to have survived? Regrettably, only one known Welsh wool quilt, now in a Kansas museum, has a sufficiently good history and provenance to suggest that it did cross the Atlantic with a Welsh family when they emigrated in the 1890s to join close family members already in Emporia, Kansas.[23] In mitigation of such slight material evidence, it must be remembered that such a low survival rate is not at all unusual amongst under-valued quilt genre. For instance, only one Australian 'convict' quilt survives of the several thousand that were probably made by the more than 12,000 female convicts transported there in the nineteenth century.[24] And, much nearer our own time, only a mere handful of quilts survive

from the thousands of Canadian Red Cross quilts (over 25,000 from Nova Scotia alone) made for relief during World War II, 1939-1945.[25]

The apparent absence of explicit documentary or material cultural evidence should not be taken as an indication that bedcovers, including quilts, were not part of the personal belongings of the more than 100,000 Welsh immigrants who entered America between 1800 and 1900. On the contrary, a strong circumstantial argument can be made for the pragmatic transfer of personal goods and Welsh quilt-making knowledge to the new American environment. For if a quarryman could be valued there for his economically useful slate-splitting skills, why should not his wife's quilting accomplishments have equally enriched their new domestic and cultural sphere?

5

Pennsylvania and Ohio: The Meeting Grounds?

*P*ENNSYLVANIA LOOMED LARGE IN NINETEENTH-CENTURY Welsh emigration history. The U.S. census of 1900, which calculated foreign-born citizens in all the different U.S. states, showed that more than 38% of the Welsh-born population in America was in Pennsylvania, whilst Ohio was the state with the next highest proportion, 12%.[1] Together, these two states accounted for half of all Welsh-born immigrants in the US at the beginning of the twentieth century, a statistic that demonstrates the major importance of these two states to incoming Welsh migrants. The U.S. censuses from 1850 (the first to indicate place of birth) confirm the 'pull' of these states for Welsh migrants, and also confirm that Welsh immigration into Pennsylvania and Ohio was ongoing throughout the nineteenth century. But, as the last chapter has shown, from the 1820s onwards Welsh immigration to America had an industrial rather than rural character, so the greater proportion of those who settled in the two states after that decade went to industrial centres where their technical skills were in great demand. Rarely did the paths of these more industrial immigrants cross those of the Amish of rural Pennsylvania, or of those Amish who had by then settled in rural Ohio.

In the post-colonial era before 1820 however, the character of Welsh settlement was rather different, more closely paralleling that of Amish communities. Both groups followed the same pioneering trails westward searching out new lands to farm, and their settlement trajectories coincided in historically-identifiable localities in Pennsylvania and Ohio. But, as families from both communities moved on from Ohio and extended into Indiana and points west, Amish and Welsh settlement patterns tended to diverge. So, although Welsh migrants settled in the same states as the Amish, the further into the American interior the two groups of migrants moved, opportunities for interaction between them appear to have lessened. However, further opportunity did arise back east in the oldest and most stable

5.1. Derelict remains of the second log church built by the Welsh community
in Ebensburg, Cambria County Pennsylvania, c. 1804,
to function as a church and also (in the upper floor) as the county courthouse.
Courtesy of Cambria County Historical Society.

of the Amish communities—that of Lancaster County, Pennsylvania—where a group of Welsh industrial migrants settled on the York County/Lancaster County boundary in the mid-nineteenth century.

Accordingly, the broad geographic and cultural focus of this chapter concentrates on those localities in Pennsylvania and Ohio where Welsh communities arose either alongside established Amish groups or, conversely, where migrating Amish families settled close to existing Welsh communities. It is only by comparing the settlement patterns of both the Amish and the Welsh across nineteenth-century America that these contiguous localities have been brought to light; it is possible that future research may yield more potentially interactive Welsh/Amish 'meeting points' than those identified and outlined here.

The Welsh in Nineteenth-century Pennsylvania

When lands in the west of Pennsylvania opened up in the years after the end of the Revolutionary War, the first new settlement established by the Welsh was in the area that was later to become Cambria County, in west-central Pennsylvania. In 1796, a group of Welsh farmers and their families left Llanbrynmair in Mid-Wales, then a 'hotspot' of Welsh religious nonconformism, intending to acquire their own land in America. Primarily a farming unit, they were led by two nonconformist ministers and established the twin settlements of Ebensburg and Beulah, with Ebensburg the centre for the Congregationalists among them and Beulah for the Welsh Baptists. Within a year they had built a church, the Welsh Independent Church, to service both denominations. But when Cambria County was created out of the northern part of Somerset County in 1804, Ebensburg was chosen as the new county seat. It became a prosperous settlement and the administrative centre for the county's governance and law. Beulah, meanwhile, dwindled into obscurity.

Settling in the north of what was still Somerset County, the early Welsh settlers farmed the district immediately around Ebensburg and extended their activities as far south as the locality that later became Johnstown—an area where the Amish community of Conemaugh (established 1767) was also farming.[2] These two communities, Welsh and

Amish, would have had characteristics broadly in common. Both groups consisted of pioneering farming families, both had strict religious codes rooted in nonconformist Protestantism, and were opposed to slavery; like Amish communities, Welsh Baptists practised adult baptism. Neither group had English as a first language; both dressed in traditional dress which was plain but practical in style. The Welsh families from Mid-Wales would almost certainly have included farmer-weavers skilled in the production of wool cloth, a skills norm for a farming family from the centre of a key Welsh, wool-producing district, and in an era still largely reliant upon cottage-based production.

As with the Amish settlements of adjacent Somerset County, the nineteenth-century census

5.2. Painting by the anonymous 'Welsh primitif' artist of an adult baptism in the River Rheidol near Aberystwyth, Mid-Wales, c. 1840.
By permission of Llyfrgell Genedlaethol Cymru/The National Library of Wales.

5.3. Painting by the anonymous 'Welsh primitif' artist
of a Mid Wales farm and water-powered mill, c.1840.
By permission of Llyfrgell Genedlaethol Cymru/The National Library of Wales.

records make it possible to trace patterns of growth and change within Cambria County's Welsh community. In 1800, when Ebensburg and Beulah were still in Somerset County, half of the population of the area around Ebensburg was Welsh. In fact, the Ebensburg-centred community accounted for three-quarters of the entire Welsh population in Somerset County itself, whilst the remaining quarter, numbering some 50 individuals, lived to the south in an area that was partly occupied by a much larger group of families with probable Amish surnames.[3]

Analysis of census data from 1800 to 1850 reveals the subsequent geographical relationship between the Welsh settlement in Cambria County and the probable Amish communities on the Cambria County/Somerset County border. They indicate that Welsh farmers were clustered around Ebensburg, with Amish farmers similarly clustered around what became Johnstown to the south. During that time, individuals with probable Amish surnames amounted to 35–65% of the population in the area in and around Johnstown.[4] The Welsh population grew only slowly at first, but as industrial developments around Ebensburg and Johnstown gathered pace, the numbers of Welsh increased rapidly. By 1850, over 65% of the 1,400 settlers in and around Ebensburg were from Welsh families that had immigrated during the past 30 years, i.e. since 1820. Overall, Welsh immigrants represented nearly three-quarters (72%) of the foreign-born population of the area in 1850, and half of these were recent incomers, settling there in the decade 1840–1850.[5]

ROBERT W. ROBERTS FAMILY
About 1890
Front Row - Rees R. Roberts, Robert W. Roberts, Rachel (Jones) Roberts, Jane (Jennie Roberts) Bumford
Back Row - Timothy Roberts, Robert S. Roberts

5.4. Robert W. Roberts and family, Cambria County Pennsylvania, c. 1890; Robert W. Roberts (2ⁿᵈ left) was born in Anglesey, North Wales in 1825 and emigrated with his family to Cambria County c. 1832 when he was six years old. *Courtesy of Cambria County Historical Society.*

The continued in-migration of Welsh settlers to the area is very significant. They reinforced the visible Welsh presence in Cambria County and their cultural character appears to have been maintained in the Ebensburg region throughout much of the nineteenth century. Even into the 1870s, the Welsh were still the largest ethnic group in Ebensburg and Cambria Township.[6] Writing in 1872, Rev. Thomas paints a picture of Ebensburg as a particularly prosperous town:

At the present time they have enough comfortable houses there. They are good, hard-working, and truly faithful people and do their best to bring up their children in the same way. The majority of its inhabitants are Welsh, and several of them are men of riches, learning, and influence. Welsh farmers have bought the land for miles around and live comfortably on it. But their lands are "running out," and many of the children are immigrating [sic] to the west...[7]

Ebensburg and Cambria County were in fact well situated for these expansionary movements west. Even before the building of the turnpike (toll road), c.1810, which ran through the centre of Ebensburg, Cambria County had became a hub for transport routes crossing from the east to Pittsburgh. Additional transport links—including railroads—followed, so Cambria County and its

5.5. Salem Welsh Calvinist Methodist Church, North Ebensburg, Cambria County Pennsylvania, built in 1880. *Courtesy of Cambria County Historical Society.*

nineteenth-century Welsh community did not remain isolated, but found themselves favorably positioned as a prosperous industrial node within a communications corridor to the west.

In southeast Pennsylvania, both York and Lancaster counties had been settled by Welsh immigrants in the eighteenth century, when families moved out to farm land beyond the original 'Welsh Tract.' It is, however, nineteenth-century Welsh immigrants to this area that have relevance for any potential cross-over activities with respect to quilt-making. The nineteenth-century Welsh influx into these two southeast Pennsylvania counties was grounded, quite literally, on the discovery of rich seams of slate which outcropped on both banks (i.e. north and south) of the Susquehanna River.

The commercial exploitation of slate began in 1800 when a Quaker, Joshua Brown, purchased Slate Hill in the Peter's Creek area of Lancaster County (on the Susquehanna's east side). He initiated a business that was to result in an influx of Welsh quarry workers skilled in the production of fine roofing slates, a product for which there was growing demand, especially in the construction of prestigious buildings.[8] Though some slate quarrying operations had also begun on the York County (west) side of the Susquehanna River, these had subsequently become dormant. But in the 1840s new quarrying leases were granted there to Welsh immigrants who brought in further compatriots

from North Wales skilled in both quarrying and slate-splitting.

By 1848, more than 75 men were employed in the York County quarries, the majority of them Welsh. Two years later, in 1850, there were 42 Welsh-born 'labourers'—presumed employees of the Peach Bottom quarries—together with their families, and the entire Welsh community numbered a little over a hundred.[9] It was this community that established the village of Bangor (later called West Bangor) and which, by 1849, had built a non-denominational chapel that was later to be followed by a Calvinist Methodist chapel (Figure 4.3) and a church for the Congregationalists.

As the original nucleus of Welsh immigrants in York County expanded, some moved across the river to work in the Lancaster County quarries of the Peter's Creek area, confusingly, in the area also known as Peach Bottom. Of this venture, Ellis and Evans' *History of Lancaster County, Pennsylvania* (1883) records:

> ... the Welsh Church near Peach Bottom [Lancaster County, was] built to accommodate the men employed in the slate quarry, who were largely of that nationality, and many of whom became permanent settlers in the surrounding country, and who desired services in their own language, and who built a house for that purpose...[10]

By 1850 the Lancaster County quarries had become the smaller of the two quarrying concerns

5.6. Four of the 'old time' Pennsylvanian-Welsh slate splitters demonstrating their craft in the late 1930s: (left to right) William W. Williams, E. E. Jones, D. H. Hughes, T. Parry. *Courtesy of Old Line Museum, Delta, York County.*

5.7. Lithograph of the Moore and McLaughlin slate quarry, Delta, York County Pennsylvania, n.d. *Courtesy of Old Line Museum, Delta, York County and Bob and Kathleen Britton.*

on the banks of the Susquehanna, and they were to remain so. The 1850 census gives 13 Welsh-born immigrants for Fulton Township, though by 1860 this had increased nearly five-fold, to 62—just over half (55%) of the foreign-born population in the township.[11] Over the river in York County, slate-quarrying had expanded across the Pennsylvania–Maryland state border as the new towns of Delta, South Delta (renamed Cardiff) and Cambria (renamed Whiteford) were built. Meanwhile, back in Lancaster County, another small Welsh community had built up in the town of Columbia (on the Susquehanna river) where a local steel rolling mill offered work to skilled Welshmen. Although Columbia's inhabitants did build a church, their community was weakened when many moved further south to join a Welsh community in Tennessee.

Nevertheless, the well recorded existence of these Welsh communities in the town of Columbia and in the slate-quarrying districts of Lancaster and York counties, confirms the visible presence of nineteenth-century Welsh immigrants on the northwest and southwest fringes of the Lancaster County Amish. And, by way of example, the cultural continuity of this Welsh presence is illustrated in the Rev. Thomas's description of the character, location, and communication links of the community in West Bangor, York County:

W. C. PARRY & Co.,
JOHN HUMPHREY & CO., QUARRY,
Lately operated by the Peach Bottom Slate Manufacturing Co.,
MANUFACTURERS OF
Peach Bottom Roofing Slate,
WEST BANGOR,
ju2 YORK COUNTY, PA.

R. L. JONES & CO.,
OLD "BIG QUARRY,"
Formerly operated by Rowland Parry and Isaac Parker & Co.
OPENED IN 1865,
Manufacturers of
Peach Bottom Roofing Slate,
WEST BANGOR,
York County, Pa.
The product of this quarry established the reputation of Peach Bottom Slate, which it has since maintained. ju2

5.8. Advertisements by Welsh-owned companies for roofing slates in the *Delta Herald*, York County Pennsylvania, April 6 1887. *Courtesy of Old Line Museum, Delta, York County.*

SLATE HILL, York Co. This place is located on the south side of the Susquehanna river near the boundary with the state of Maryland ... One is able to get to it on the stage every other day from Lancastar [sic] or on the train from Philadelphia to Havre de Grace and from there by carriage or by the boats on the river or the canal. It is an old place and consists of agricultural land for the most part. But slate was discovered and the quarries were opened and worked by the Welsh who then had a strong settlement there ... Three Welsh churches were established there ... Perhaps there are now [c. 1870] 600 people ... The village there is small, there are two Welsh chapels, some

5.9. Shank's Ferry at Peach Bottom, York County Pennsylvania, c. 1910; this ferry was one of three passenger ferries which crossed the Susquehanna River between York County and Lancaster County, a service which ceased in 1925. *Courtesy of Old Line Museum, Delta, York County.*

STEAMBOAT FERRY,

PEACH BOTTOM, PA.

———

REGULAR TRIPS:

Leave York County Shore 8:30 a. m., 1:45 and 6:00 p. m.

Leave Lancaster County Shore 7:45 and 11:30 a. m., 4:45 p. m.

"   "   "   " *9/5 W M*

CONNECTS WITH PASSENGER TRAINS ON C. AND P. D. R. R.

AND I. O. AND S. R. R.

EXTRA TRIPS TO SUIT THE TRAVEL.

WM. SHANK, MANAGER.

5.10. Ferry schedule for Shank's Ferry, c. 1900. *Courtesy of Old Line Museum, Delta, York County.*

stores, and not a single tavern! [emphasis as in original][12]

Not to be confused with its Lancaster County namesake, Thomas's description of "SLATE HILL, York Co." confirms the retention of a Welsh cultural framework. Welsh temperance lived on, as did other aspects of Welsh nonconformist life. As well as places of worship, traditional Welsh vernacular housing was built to house the quarryworkers and their families, with some examples surviving today (Figure 5.11). By the 1880s, the Welsh population was holding regular *Eisteddfod* to celebrate Welsh culture, though whether the gender-based art of Welsh quilt-making had any part in that cultural celebration is not recorded, and no Welsh quilts are known to survive from this southern Pennsylvanian community. It is an unfortunate fact of historical life that stone-built, slate-roofed dwellings are much more likely to survive than the domestic textiles that they sheltered.

5.11. Cottages at Coulsontown, near Delta, York County Pennsylvania, built by Welsh immigrants between 1845 and 1860 in vernacular Welsh style, and now listed on the National Register of Historic Places. *Courtesy of Old Line Museum, Delta, York County.*

The Welsh in Nineteenth-century Ohio

The first Welsh settlers arrived in Ohio just as the nineteenth century began. Two of the original prospectors for the Welsh settlement in Somerset/Cambria County (Pennsylvania) moved on to Ohio after just five years in the Allegheny Mountains. Purchasing fertile land in Butler County, southwest Ohio (a little to the north of Cincinnati), they founded the Welsh settlement known as "Paddy's Run" in 1801, at an area now known as Shandon (see Figure 5.12). The settlement thrived and continued to attract Welsh immigrant farmers for many decades. Interestingly, Butler County was also the location of a Hessian Amish settlement in the 1830s, although this was one of the nineteenth-century Amish settlements that did not survive as a conservative Amish community after the 1860s schisms.

As an off-shoot of the Somerset/Cambria County settlement, the Paddy's Run venture acted as something of an agricultural beacon for, once Welsh farmers in Pennsylvania became aware of the fertility of land to the west, 'Ohio Fever' set in and some began to search for productive land there.

As a result, the descriptively-named 'Welsh Hills' settlement was established in Licking County, central Ohio, in 1802, only a year after that at Paddy's Run (see map in Figure 5.13). It too became a favored locality for putative immigrant farmers and, by 1870, there were an estimated 2,500 Welsh inhabitants in the area.[13] Fortuitously, a remarkable description of this Welsh Hills settlement was penned in the 1860s, not by a Welshman but by a Virginian-born civic leader of German origin, Isaac Smucker. A member of the Lutheran church, Smucker had spent five of his younger years in Somerset County, Pennsylvania, before moving to Newark, Ohio, and he appears to have had considerable cross-cultural empathy with the Welsh, referring to them as "our pioneer friends." He described the difficulties faced by these Welsh

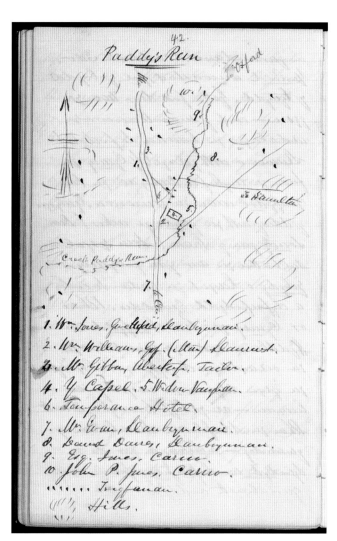

5.12. Early nineteenth-century sketch map of the Welsh settlement of Paddy's Run, Butler County Ohio, founded in 1801. *By permission of Llyfrgell Genedlaethol Cymru/The National Library of Wales (Wales-Ohio Project).*

5.13. Nineteenth century Welsh settlements in Ohio together with nineteenth-century spread of Amish settlement; the earliest Welsh settlements are dated.

Key to abbreviations:

W = counties with Welsh settlements,
A = counties with Amish settlements;
Ada = Adams Co.;
Bel = Belmont Co.;
Car = Carroll Co.;
Cha = Champaign Co.;
Cos = Coshocton Co.;
Cuy = Cuyahoga Co.;
Def = Defiance Co;
Fai = Fairfield Co.;
Fra = Franklin Co.;

Fu = Fulton Co.;
Gue = Guernsey Co.;
Ham = Hamilton Co.;
Har = Hardin Co.;
Har = Harrison Co.;
High = Highland Co.;
Jef = Jefferson Co.;
Kno = Knox Co.;
Log = Logan Co.;
Mei = Meigs Co.;
Mon = Monroe Co.;

Mor = Morrow Co.;
Mus = Muskingum Co.;
Per = Perry Co.;
Put = Putnam Co;
Sta = Stark Co.;
Sum = Summit Co.;
Vin = Vinton Co.;
Way = Wayne Co.

Data sources: Crowley, 1978;
Hartman, 1983; and Van Vugt, 1999.

5.14. Thomas Watkins and Jane Evans Watkins of Gomer, Allen County Ohio;
Thomas was one of the three pioneers from Paddy's Run, Butler County who,
in 1833, founded the Welsh settlement in northwest Ohio that later became Gomer.
*By permission of Llyfrgell Genedlaethol Cymru/The National Library of Wales
(Wales-Ohio Project) and Allen County Historical Society.*

settlers who, like their European neighbors, had "but a limited knowledge of the English language", and he made particular comment on their religious fervor:

> [In the Welsh hills] the descendants of the early settlers, together with many other of their countrymen, more recent immigrants, still live, their Welsh habits and characteristics, though somewhat modified, still predominate ... Our Welsh pioneers and their descendants, as well as the present population of Licking County, may be characterized as pre-eminently religious ... Probably a larger portion of them are church-goers, church members, than ... any other class or nationality of our population, native or foreign.[14]

In the adjacent county of Delaware another Welsh settlement soon followed that of the Welsh Hills community in central Ohio, so when the Amish arrived in the state around 1808–09 the Welsh settlements of Paddy's Run, Welsh Hills and Delaware County were already well established. Though the outbreak of the 1812 War temporarily put an end to this particular era of settlement, that interregnum was followed (in 1818) by the founding of further new Welsh communities in Gallia and Jackson counties in southeastern Ohio. Each year of the next decade, the 1820s, saw new Welsh farming families arriving in Ohio direct from Wales, most of them settling within their ethnic groups. But by the 1830s these relatively new communities were already outstripping their available resources of land and, in just the same way that the Amish established offshoots, Welsh daughter colonies were also set up. One grew as a daughter colony from Paddy's Run. Located in Allen County in northwest Ohio, it was named Gomer. Similarly, another 1830s Welsh settlement began in Portage County, northeast Ohio, to be followed in the 1840s by another in Van Wert County on the western border of the state.

Throughout the first half of the nineteenth century and beyond, Welsh farming settlements in Ohio continued to receive new Welsh immigrants, and this despite the fact that inexpensive new farming land was becoming available in the states further west. Paddy's Run in Butler County, its daughter colony of Gomer in Allen County, and the Welsh Hills settlement of Licking County were particular magnets. Thanks to the German Isaac Smucker, the powerful contemporary description of the Licking County settlement has survived, one that evokes the continued 'Welshness' of that community. There is no reason to suppose that the cultural and religious values, and cultural identity, of other nineteenth-century Welsh farming communities in Ohio were any different in intensity. It is therefore appropriate to consider the extent to which the Amish in Ohio and Pennsylvania were aware of the ethnic Welsh, their religiosity, and their way of life.

JOSIAH JONES (Josiah Brynmair).

5.15. Josiah Jones, farmer, undertaker, and composer of hymns and carols of Gomer, Allen County Ohio; Josiah was born in 1807 in Llanbrynmair, Mid Wales and emigrated to America with his wife and children in 1850.
By permission of Llyfrgell Genedlaethol Cymru/The National Library of Wales (Wales-Ohio Project).

5.16. William W. Roberts and family at the family farm in Gomer, Allen County Ohio; William's father Thomas had emigrated to America from Llanbrynmair, Mid Wales to Paddy's Run, Butler County Ohio, but moved to Gomer in 1839 to become a farmer.
By permission of Llyfrgell Genedlaethol Cymru/The National Library of Wales (Wales-Ohio Project) and Kay Studer.

Welsh Settlement and Amish-Welsh Interaction

However well-documented the general history of the Welsh settlements in Pennsylvania and Ohio may now be, the extent to which Welsh communities interacted with their neighbors, particularly with Amish neighbors at a person-to-person and gender level, remains enigmatic. That the Welsh piqued the close attention and admiration of a man like Isaac Smucker seems to indicate that the Welsh communities had a level of outreach beyond the boundaries of their own ethnic group, or just that of their British compatriots. Regrettably though, dedicated accounts such as Smucker's are rare.

Anecdotal evidence from south-eastern Pennsylvania does suggest that some faith-based interaction did take place. In one reputedly early nineteenth-century instance, contact and co-operation was said to have occurred between Welsh nonconformists and the Amish Mennonites in the north of Chester County, close to the Chester/Lancaster boundary:

> There was an old church/school near Malvern known as the "Flat Road Amish Mennonite Church." ... It was also used at the same time by the 7th Day Baptists (usually Welshmen) for worship. The Amish Mennonites worshipping on Sunday and the other group on Saturday. Both seemed to have educated their children together in the same church/school building and buried in the same cemetery.[15]

Unsupported anecdotal evidence of this kind must be treated with caution, and requires corroboration and clarification. But, if true in substance, then such an account clearly suggests a sympathetic relationship between some Anabaptists and Welsh groups and, at the very least, it indicates the acceptance of historic opportunities for interaction at the local level.

What the formal historiography proves beyond doubt, however, is that the Welsh and Amish did live side-by-side in the Cambria County/Somerset County of west-central Pennsylvania in the first half of the nineteenth century and beyond; and that there was a continued influx of migrants from Wales into this area as nineteenth-century industrialization gathered pace. It also recognizes and describes the size and visibility of the Welsh community within that area, emphasizing the significance of the locale as a transport hub through which west-bound migrants traveled. In that same 1800–1850 period, sources also show that Welsh settlements proliferated in Ohio as farmers from Pennsylvania established new settlements there that, in turn, attracted immigrants direct from Wales. Significantly, all of these Welsh settlements were in counties that either hosted small Amish settlements or, in terms of travel, were proximate to the main Ohio Amish settlement centred on Holmes County (see map in Figure 5.13).

Historical documentation also conclusively demonstrates that, after a significant immigration of Welsh slate-workers into Pennsylvania beginning in the 1840s, there were strong, visible Welsh settlements in the southeast of that state, in York and Lancaster Counties (i.e. on both sides of the Susquehanna River). Chronologically and culturally, it is important to note that this dedicated influx of Welsh quarrymen and their families came from a Welsh milieu in which quilt-making had become an established vernacular craft. So wool quilts, in the deep-dyed colors of traditional Welsh style, would likely have been among their possessions. In addition, after arrival they created economically-successful, resource-based communities that persisted in situ throughout the remainder of the nineteenth century, thus maintaining a fluctuating and mobile Welsh population in close proximity to the Lancaster County Amish. So neither cultural group was an ephemeral presence there.

The key objective of this chapter has been to clarify areas of Welsh settlement in nineteenth-century America that were close enough to Amish settlements to allow for cultural cross-over in relation to quilt-making. The historical evidence confirms that visible and recognizably Welsh communities lived side-by-side with Amish communities in a number of areas of Pennsylvania and Ohio during the mid-nineteenth century, the period when Amish quilt-making is presumed to have evolved. It is certainly likely that incoming Welsh migrants would have brought quilts. As bedding, wool quilts were commonplace possessions in Welsh working-class households throughout the nineteenth century. Given the continued in-migration of the Welsh, it is hard to conceive that some wool quilts in vernacular style did not find their way into the nineteenth-century homes of Welsh-Americans. Whether Welsh women continued quilt-making within a Welsh cultural framework once living in America is another question, but knowledge of that tradition and the production of wool cloth cannot help but have travelled with them, and was part of some incomers' cultural vocabulary.

Amish and Welsh Quilts: Individualistic or Imitative?

*T*HE CENTRAL QUESTION AT THE HEART of the debate about the relationship between Amish and Welsh quilts is whether the similarities that visually connect these quilts can be interpreted as being purely coincidental—the result of spontaneous, independent developments on either side of the Atlantic at similar points in time—or whether they signal a cultural cross-over in design style through social interaction between Amish and Welsh communities. This chapter will focus on an examination of these much-debated visual similarities in order to determine how closely individual characteristics can be correlated between the two quilt genres. Crucially, such a comparative analysis can now be set in the context of Amish society and settlement in nineteenth-century America, and the relationship between Amish settlements and the new Welsh-American communities that formed following the nineteenth-century wave of Welsh immigration. When viewed in this context, some of the unresolved questions relating to the early development of Amish quilt-making take on a different perspective, and can be viewed though a broader historical frame of reference.

But first, to the quilts—the surviving material culture that provoked the original question of cultural cross-over. Now that the histories of these two quilt-making traditions have been charted, it will be clear that it is Welsh vernacular or 'folk-style' quilts, most especially wool (or flannel) quilts, on which the characteristics that hallmark Amish quilts can also be found. Objective comparisons of nineteenth-century Amish quilts with this group of Welsh quilts from the same period (hereafter 'Welsh quilts') are generally considered to reveal four generic characteristics:

(1) the use of fabrics dyed in deep, often jewel-like colors;

(2) the use of plain rather than printed cloth;

(3) quilt tops pieced in symmetrical abstract designs of large fabric shapes; and

(4) extensive quilting designs, sometimes ornate in character, worked through the quilt layers.

But these particular characteristics are not shared by all Amish and Welsh quilts. There are stronger links between Welsh quilts and those made by the Lancaster County Old Order Amish than between Welsh quilts and Amish quilts from the Midwest, with the exception of quilts from Illinois.

Connections in Color and Cloth

The two characteristics that nineteenth-century Amish quilts from both Lancaster County and the Midwest do share with Welsh quilts, however, are:

(1) the use of plain cloth; and

(2) an overall dark color palette.

And the comparisons of cloth and color go further. In both quilt genres, woolen fabrics were used at specific points in the nineteenth century. For Welsh quilts, the indigenous resource of woolen cloth was used throughout the nineteenth century and beyond, though cotton increasingly replaced wool as the fabric of choice (Figure 6.1); after the period of World War I (1914–1918) few wool quilts were made.

The use of woolen cloth for Lancaster County Amish quilts (hereafter 'Lancaster quilts') has long been recognized as a contributing factor to the aesthetic quality of this particular genre, but surviving Midwest Amish quilts also show that wool was used in the earliest phase of Amish quilt-making in some Midwest states. The quilt in Figure 6.2 from Indiana is one example, and the Amish quilt collection in Illinois State Museum includes several wool quilts from the second half of the nineteenth century (Figures 3.4 and 3.5). Whether these early Amish wool quilts were regarded as quilts, or as comforters or haps, is a question that was addressed in Chapter 3.

As with Welsh quilts, cotton eventually replaced wool for most Amish quilts, but it was a process that had uneven progression. By the 1880s, many of the Midwest Amish quilts were pieced in plain cottons and, by the turn of the twentieth century, cotton had almost entirely replaced wool. For Illinois Amish quilts, the use of woolen fabrics persisted longer than in other Midwest states as it also did in Lancaster County, where even 1920s and 1930s quilts incorporate wool or wool-mix fabrics (Figure 6.3). When set in the context of the nineteenth-century history of the Lancaster County Amish, this may represent a conservative trait as this particular Amish group became less connected through family ties to Amish communities beyond Pennsylvania (see Chapter 3).

Whether in wool or cotton, the color palettes of nineteenth-century Amish and Welsh quilts are strikingly similar. Both are characterized by the use of deep-dyed fabrics in dense, saturated colors. Though both Amish and Welsh quilts may assume an overall sombre hue, they can include dramatic color combinations and accents of softer and lighter tones. For Welsh wool quilts, surviving examples show no particular regional variations in terms of color; instead, they reflect a local industry which produced dull but practical work-wear, a wide range of colors for military uniforms, and fabrics for traditional Welsh dress including stripes and checks as well as plain weaves (Figure 6.4). The spark in a significantly high proportion of Welsh quilts comes from the inclusion of that fabric so emblematic of Wales—red flannel—but other contrasts within an overall blue-brown-grey-black palette can include purple, maroon, magenta, electric blue, and pink as can be seen in the quilts in Figures 6.5, 6.6 and 6.7. Red flannel is not infrequently found combined with blue, a popular two-tone combination seen in the quilt in Figure 6.8, which presents an interesting comparison to the Amish quilt in Figure 6.9.

Though Amish quilts show a degree of regional variation in color, with Midwestern quilters generally using more black than Pennsylvanian

6.1. Center Diamond cotton quilt, Welsh, Pontrhydfendigaid, Cardiganshire, 1890–1900. 74" x 84" (188cm x 214cm). *Courtesy of Jen Jones Quilts; photography by Roger Clive-Powell.*

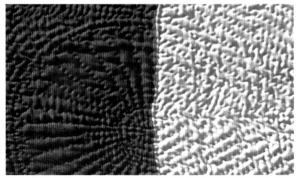

6.2. Block quilt, Unequal Nine-patch, wool, Amish, believed to have been made by a member of the Bontrager family in the 1880s, LaGrange, Indiana, 61" x 76" (155 cm x 193 cm).
From the Collection of the Indiana State Museum and Historic Sites.

6.3. Center Diamond wool quilt, Amish, Lancaster County Pennsylvania,
initialled 'IL', c. 1925, 77" x 77" (195 cm x 195 cm).
Courtesy of The Heritage Center of Lancaster County.

6.4. Detail of a scrap quilt, Welsh, pieced from striped
fabrics woven for use in traditional Welsh petticoats.
Courtesy Quilt Association, Minerva Arts Centre.

6.5. Center Medallion wool quilt, made by Elizabeth Howells Beynon,
St Clears, Carmarthenshire, South West Wales,
c. 1850, 76" x 85" (193 cm x 216 cm).
Courtesy of St Fagans: National History Museum, Wales.

6.6. Center Medallion quilt, Welsh,
stitched both by hand and machine by weaver Benjamin Jones
(or a member of his family) from off-cuts from Ogof Mill, Drefach-Felindre,
South West Wales, late nineteenth century, 70" x 83" (178 cm x 210 cm).
Courtesy of St Fagans: National History Museum, Wales.

6.7. Center Medallion quilt, Welsh,
stitched both by hand and machine by weaver Benjamin Jones
(or a member of his family) from off-cuts from Ogof Mill, Drefach-Felindre,
South West Wales, late nineteenth century, 76" x 86" (193 cm x 218 cm).
Courtesy of St Fagans: National History Museum, Wales.

6.8. Pin-wheel quilt in red and blue wool, Cardiganshire,
c. 1875; for full quilt, see Figure 2.15.
Courtesy of Jen Jones Quilts; photography by Roger Clive-Powell.

6.9. Bars quilt in red and blue cottons, Amish,
believed to have been made by a member of the Yoder family,
1900-1930, LaGrange County, Indiana, 70" x 92" (178 cm x 234 cm).
From the Collection of the Indiana State Museum and Historic Sites.

quilters, the characteristic that both traditions share is an overall broadening of color use as the early phase of Amish quilt-making gave way to the classic era. In her study of Lancaster County Amish quilts, Herr concisely summarized the changing use of color in the quilts from this south-eastern corner of Pennsylvania:

> The colors of [the] top fabrics ... changed with time. Early quilts tended to have less color variety ... Brown and darker shades of blues and greens were predominant in pre-1900 examples ... Later in the 1930s hot pinks and bright lavenders appeared along with lighter colors ... Bold and vivid red, blue, turquoise, green and purple were expertly combined by Amish women from the 1920s on. Occasionally in later 1930s and 1940s quilts, one sees small blocks of plain yellow and white, but not in overwhelming quantity.[1]

But in widening their choice of color, the Lancaster County Amish may once again have lagged behind their Midwest counterparts. The dated quilt in Figure 6.10, made in Ohio in 1888, shows a wide mix of colors including turquoise, bright green, and a sharp yellow fabric that sparkles near the centre of each block. This Ohio quilt also features red fabrics, including a perhaps surprising use of an eye-catching, arresting red, a color not uncommon on early Amish quilts. Examples can also be seen in the quilts in Figures 3.5 and 3.8, with the fabrics in the quilt in Figure 3.5 amongst the few fabrics on Amish quilts thought to be hand-woven and dyed with natural colors.[2] As noted above, red is the single most commonly used color on nineteenth-century Welsh quilts.

Color and cloth in Amish quilts have been widely interpreted as encoding the belief structures of Amish society with its emphasis on humility, modesty, and plainness, and its strictures on fashion and frivolity. Such controls were first imposed on the visual symbols of the group, particularly Amish dress, by Jakob Amman, the sect's founder. But the link between Amish quilts and Amish dress was practical as well as ethical. In the nineteenth-

century, Amish women made almost all the clothing required by their families. Once quilts began to be made in Amish communities, fabrics were acquired with both dress-making and quilt-making in mind so that off-cuts and additional lengths of clothing fabrics could be incorporated into quilts.[3]

The extensive literature on Amish quilts clarifies the extent to which the use of color and cloth in Amish quilts was underpinned by the ethos of a controlled, faith-based society and underscores the relationship between quilts and Amish dress codes. But much of this work relates to phases of Amish quilt-making in twentieth-century America, and the extent to which similar interpretations can be placed on fabric use in the early development of Amish quilt-making remains unclear. It was shown in Chapter 3 that many of the visual markers that now distinguish Amish communities from mainstream society, and separate one Amish community from another, were not in place in the mid-nineteenth century. There is no evidence to show that there was significant outward distinction between the Amish and non-Amish in terms of dress at that point in time. If there was little distinction in the dress of Amish and non-Amish Americans in the nineteenth century, why should the Amish apparently develop a quilt style that appears to represent a separation in color and cloth from mainstream American quilt-making? There is evidence that the more 'tradition-minded' Amish eschewed the use of patterned dress materials,[4] the fabrics commonly employed in mainstream American quilt-making, so perhaps when they turned to quilt-making, these Amish quilt-makers found a model to follow that used plain rather than printed cloth.

Although nineteenth-century Welsh communities were, like the Amish, deeply religious, color and cloth in Welsh quilts were not bounded by ethical restrictions, so far as is known. But as well as incorporating the products of local industry, they do reflect the colors and cloths of traditional Welsh dress—a visual representation of national rather than religious identity—and the glowing quality of the reds, blues, greens, and purples that resonate from Welsh wool quilts is testimony to the skills of generations of Welsh dyers. There is little doubt that Welsh quilters

6.10. Detail of Block quilt, Railroad Crossing, Amish,
made by Melinda Miller of Walnut Creek, Ohio; for full quilt see Figure 1.9.
©From the collection of Faith and Stephen Brown.

were using deep-dyed plain fabric for quilt-making well before the Amish established their own quilt-making tradition.

Of themselves, the shared characteristics of a dark and dramatic color palette combined with plain cloth are not unique. Other quilt genres, such as the nineteenth-century British 'clothograms' and the nineteenth-century silk quilts pieced by Pennsylvanian Quakers, also share these characteristics. But, in their separate ways, both of these quilt genres have different characters to Amish quilts. The British 'clothograms' and the wider group of European 'Intarsia' patchworks are a gender-oriented genre of pictorial imagery and intricate craftsmanship. The pieced silk Quaker quilts from Pennsylvania use a fabric with social symbolism that, however plain, signaled a quiet affluence. The minimalist style, robust character, and particular aesthetic of Amish quilts, however, appear to have much in common with Welsh quilts, a commonality that has resulted in misidentifications.

Connections in Design

Turning to the design formats of Amish and Welsh quilts, the designs with which early and classic Amish quilts were pieced together show a more marked degree of regional variation than is evidenced in their use of color. Even from their earliest beginnings, quilts from the Midwest states of Ohio and Indiana, the first states to be settled by Amish communities in the westward migration from Pennsylvania, appear to have had a strong and ongoing association with the pieced block styles that characterize America's mainstream tradition of quilt-making. One of the earliest Indiana Amish quilts, signed and dated 1875, is a classic 'on point' block design that is rooted in the vibrant nineteenth-century American tradition of pieced-block quilts (Figure 1.10), rather than referencing the simpler and more restricted block styles of the nineteenth-century British tradition. That Midwest Amish quilt-makers drew on the American pieced-block tradition from at least the last quarter of the nineteenth century has been well-documented. Research has also confirmed that Midwest Amish quilters not only drew on the American visual tradition but, in addition, accessed American printed pattern sources as early as the late 1880s.[5]

By contrast, historic Amish quilts from Lancaster County, Pennsylvania appear to be more divorced from the American pieced-quilt tradition. The precise geometry of their large planes of cloth in abstract design has little in common with mainstream American quilt-making of the same period, with its stereotypical design sets of block-pieced patterns. Though basic Center Medallion styles, like Center Diamond, had been used in American quilt-making in the late 1700s and early 1800s, they had not usually been pieced in the pared-down, unadorned style which developed amongst the Old Order Amish of Lancaster County towards the end of the nineteenth century. At that time, the Center Medallion style of piecing, with its Center Diamond variations, was no longer fashionable in high-style quilt-making either in America or in Britain. It did, however, remain a popular design style within the regional quilt-making traditions in Britain, most especially in Wales where Center Diamond designs, like that in Figure 6.11, bear the closest of comparisons with Lancaster County Amish quilts that use such a directly comparable format (Figure 6.12). Evidence for the use of this simple form of Center Diamond design in Wales—throughout the nineteenth century and across the social spectrum—is given by its use on the high-status quilt in Figure 2.2, dated 1818, and on the quilts shown in Figures 2.3 and 2.4. There can be no doubt that the use of this reductive form of the Center Diamond design on Welsh quilts preceded its use on Amish quilts.

Of the other design formats evident on Lancaster quilts, several have close parallels with designs on Welsh quilts. Center Square (Figures 6.13, 6.14 and 6.15), Bars (Strippy) quilts, and Bars variations (Figures 6.16, 6.17 and 6.18), are common to both traditions, as indeed are Wholecloth quilts (Figures 6.19 and 3.11). But these design styles have a lengthy history in the nineteenth-century quilt-making traditions of both Britain and America on broader social and geographic levels, so a direct comparison between the Amish and Welsh forms is blurred by this wider history. Only in their use of plain color and wool cloth are the Bars and Center Square quilts produced by the Lancaster Amish directly comparable with Welsh quilts of the same style, rather than to earlier American forms of these designs.

6.11. Center Diamond cotton quilt, Welsh, Pembrokeshire, c. 1880, 82" x 95" (208 cm x 241 cm). *Courtesy Quilt Association, Minerva Arts Centre; photography by Roger Clive-Powell.*

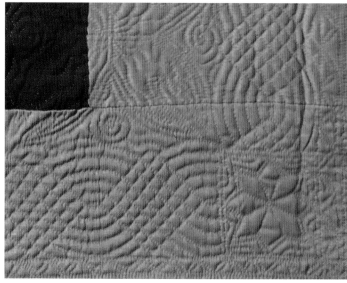

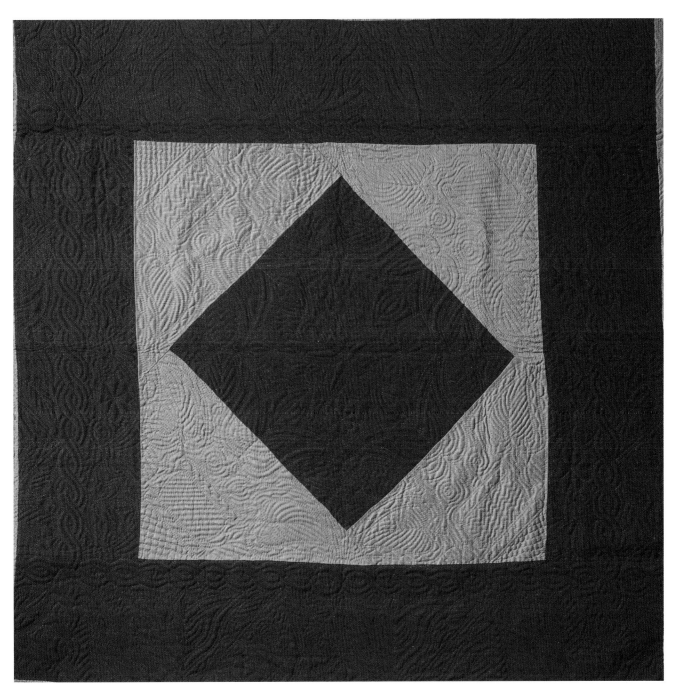

6.11a. Center Diamond, detail.
Courtesy Quilt Association, Minerva Arts Centre;
photography by Roger Clive-Powell.

6.12. Center Diamond wool quilt, Amish, probably Pennsylvania, c. 1900, 80" x 81" (203 cm x 206 cm).
Courtesy of the International Quilt Study Center & Museum, University of Nebraska–Lincoln, 2003.003.0100.

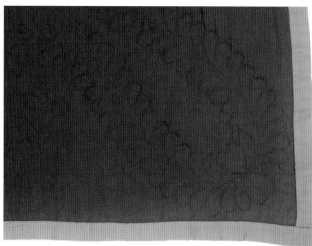

6.13. Center Square wool quilt, Welsh, probably made in Breconshire, South Wales, c. 1870, 62" x 81" (157 cm x 206 cm).
Courtesy of Jen Jones Quilts; photography by Roger Clive-Powell.

6.14. Center Square wool quilt, Welsh,
Carmarthenshire, South West Wales,
c. 1900, 74" x 85" (188 cm x 216 cm).
Courtesy of Jen Jones Quilts;
photography by Roger Clive-Powell.

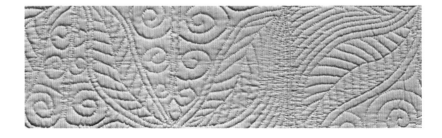

6.15. Center Square cotton quilt, Amish, probably made in Pennsylvania, c. 1880–90, 73" x 81" (185 cm x 206 cm).
Courtesy of the International Quilt Study Center & Museum, University of Nebraska–Lincoln, 2003.003.0104.

6.16. Strippy wool quilt, Welsh, Gower peninsula, South Wales, c. 1890, 82" x 88" (208 cm x 222 cm).
Courtesy of Jen Jones Quilts;
photography by Roger Clive-Powell.

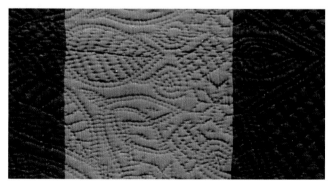

6.17. Bars wool quilt, Amish, Lancaster County Pennsylvania,
marked 'JSB/1925,' 74" x 81" (188 cm x 206 cm).
Courtesy of The Heritage Center of Lancaster County.

6.18. Bars variation, Nine Patch in Bars, Lancaster County Pennsylvania,
c. 1915, 76" x 77" (193 cm x 195 cm).
© *From the collection of Faith and Stephen Brown.*

6.19. Wholecloth quilt in red flannel,
Welsh, Gorsgoch, Carmarthenshire,
c. 1890. 77" x 84" (196 cm x 214 cm).
Courtesy of Jen Jones Quilts;
photography by Roger Clive-Powell.

One group of nineteenth-century Amish quilts are an eclectic mix of design styles which Shaw has described as combining "elements of Lancaster and Midwestern Amish traditions into a unique mix all of their own."[6] Amish quilts from Illinois vary from simple block formats and minimalist variations of strip-set styles to looser more improvisational quilts, some of which follow a basic Center Medallion format. The quilt in Figure 6.20, for example, is one of three wool quilts with large central block designs in the Illinois State Museum collection. Though seemingly synthesizing elements of the Midwest and Lancaster County traditions, to the informed British eye some of these quilt designs have an affinity with similar formats on Welsh quilts (see Figure 6.21), as well as to the general stock of nineteenth-century vernacular quilt-making in Britain.

When analyzing the quilting designs stitched onto nineteenth-century Amish and Welsh quilts, quilt-makers from both traditions undoubtedly invested considerable time and skill in the quilted element of surface design. Considered overall, the quilting designs on Amish quilts from the Midwest are competent and workmanlike rather than stylish. By contrast, the quilting designs on Lancaster quilts evolved into a handful of graceful formats which, though never achieving the high-style elaboration of eighteenth- and nineteenth-century 'white-work' (all-white Wholecloth quilts), are elegantly-constructed, fluid designs that contrast sharply with the basic outline or allover quilting often seen on American pieced-block quilts.

Like the designs of their quilt tops, the quilting designs on the quilts from Illinois do not always conform to the trends evident in the other Midwest states or in the Lancaster tradition. Although many early and classic Illinois quilts incorporate feather, cable and vine-based patterns stitched into pieced blocks and borders, as in other Amish quilts, some of the nineteenth- and early twentieth-century Illinois quilts feature a characteristic typical of British quilts. For example, the quilt in Figure 1.7 (and see back in Figure 6.22) has a quilting design that does not follow the structured geometry of the pieced design but is superimposed onto the quilt top, a design disposition that is a common feature on British quilts, including the Welsh quilts in Figures 6.11 and 6.16. It is a characteristic also seen on Pennsylvanian quilts, most

particularly on a red and blue wool quilt pieced with a large central star, dated to around 1850, and given a Somerset County provenance,[7] and on the quilt in Figure 1.4. Several other Illinois Amish quilts are quilted in a strip format with an alternating sequence of different quilting patterns running down the quilt, a format not usually employed on mainstream American quilts but one which is common on British vernacular quilts. Though the Illinois quilts have a narrow quilted border around the strip design, there is a commonality in the disposition of these strip quilting designs in the way that they are set on Illinois quilts which bears close comparison to some British vernacular quilts.

On nineteenth-century Welsh quilts, the quality of quilt stitchery can range from the exquisite Pembrokeshire quilting designs seen on the cotton quilts in Figures 2.9 and 6.11 to crudely stitched formless designs worked into thick and heavy wool quilts. Though some examples follow a strip format similar to that found on quilts from northern England,[8] most Welsh quilting follows the conservative and long-standing quilting template of border frames enclosing a central field with a center design—the classic form of British quilting that emanated from professional eighteenth-century workshops and was assimilated into nineteenth-century British vernacular style. It is this medallion-centred design style, with its large circular central pattern, which is shown in each of the four quilting designs in Figures 6.23, 6.24, 6.25 and 6.26; it is a style paralleled in the circular-centred quilting designs of both Lancaster County and Illinois quilts.

Focusing on the detail of the quilting designs— on the individual pattern elements that make up the overall design—points up differences in pattern use and disposition between Amish and Welsh quilts. None of the characteristic quilting patterns that came to hallmark Welsh quilting has so far been identified on Amish quilts from either Pennsylvania or the Midwest. Nor has the characteristic mismatch between pieced design and quilting design, so common on Welsh quilts and on British quilts as a whole, been generally recognized, save for the Illinois and Pennsylvania exceptions. So in terms of pattern detail, Amish quilters seem to have largely drawn on American-style patterns and quilting templates rather than characteristic Welsh forms.

6.20. Center Medallion wool quilt with Monkey Wrench block center,
Amish, made by Anna Swartzentruber Yoder, Illinois,
57" x 72" (145 cm x 183 cm). *Courtesy of Illinois State Museum.*

6.21. Center Medallion wool quilt with Eight-pointed Star block center,
Welsh, Ceredigion, late nineteenth century.
Courtesy of National Woollen Museum, Wales.

6.22. Back of Amish Block quilt in Figure 1.7 showing strip quilting design.
Courtesy of Illinois State Museum.

300mm

62.451
(Quarter Pattern)

6.23. One-quarter section of Medallion-centred quilting design on a cotton patchwork quilt made by Anne Williams, a maltster's wife of Llandeilo, Carmarthenshire, South West Wales, early nineteenth century; full quilt size 82" x 100" (208 cm x 253 cm). *Courtesy of St Fagans: National History Museum, Wales.*

36.191/23
(Quarter Pattern)

300 mm

6.24. One-quarter section of Medallion-centred quilting design on a cotton patchwork quilt made by Mrs Ellis of Aberystwyth, Mid Wales, mid nineteenth century:
full quilt size 73" x 87" (186 cm x 220 cm).
Courtesy of St Fagans: National History Museum, Wales.

61.113
(Quarter Pattern)

6.25. One-quarter section of Medallion-centred quilting design on a cotton patchwork quilt made by Mary Morgans of Cardigan, South West Wales, late nineteenth century; full quilt size 66" x 87" (167 cm x 221cm). *Courtesy of St Fagans: National History Museum, Wales.*

16.305
(Quarter Pattern)

6.26. One quarter section of Medallion-centred quilting design on a cotton patchwork quilt probably made in Methyr Tydfil, South Wales, late nineteenth century: full quilt size 81" x 81" (204 cm x 205 cm)
Courtesy of St Fagans: National History Museum, Wales.

Individualistic or Imitative?

Comparing the design styles of nineteenth-century Amish and Welsh quilts has revealed some clear distinctions between the extent to which Amish quilts from the Midwest and Amish quilts from the Lancaster tradition correlate with Welsh quilts. Though all Amish quilts share a color palette with Welsh quilts, together with the use of plain cloth, the pieced and quilting designs on Amish quilts from most Midwest states were drawn from the dynamic quilt-making tradition of nineteenth-century America, at least in the last quarter of that century. For the pieced designs, there is conclusive evidence that this was so.

The Lancaster quilts, and those from Illinois, tell a different story. The strong regional style which developed in Lancaster County was initially based on pieced designs of large fabric shapes joined in abstract symmetry, all of which have direct parallels with nineteenth-century Welsh quilts—most notably the Center Diamond design. Of all Amish quilt designs, the Center Diamond is the most renowned; it is the design form on which the reputation and artistic status of the Amish quilt was largely built. The sparse geometry, formulaic structure, and austere form of this design have little connection to either Midwest Amish quilt design styles or to mainstream American designs of the post-1850 period. As a quilt form, it had been considered unique in its simplicity and rigor, and "peculiar" to Lancaster County.[9] Yet this quilt design appeared in Wales in the early nineteenth century, well before Amish quilt-making apparently began. It is undoubtedly true that the geometric device of setting one square on point within another, then adding frames, has been used as ornamentation on a multiplicity of global artefacts dating back to prehistoric times, and on other early nineteenth-century American quilts. But the character, proportionalities and disposition of the design shapes and borders of this design in Welsh quilts and in Lancaster quilts, coupled with the use of wool cloth in intense color combinations, raise questions of visual imitation.

The diverse mix of pieced designs and quilting designs evident on Illinois Amish quilts also raises questions. Design dispositions like the mis-match of pieced design with quilting design and the use of large central pieced blocks have a distinctly Welsh 'feel' which, when allied to the use of plain wool cloth in an overall dark color palette, suggest an association that goes beyond the coincidental. Since the mother community of the Illinois Amish was in Somerset County Pennsylvania, in a locality with a strong nineteenth-century Welsh presence just to the north, there is an argument for Welsh influence in the development of the Illinois group of Amish quilts.

There is, then, an apparent dichotomy in the design influences that resulted in the characteristic styles of the Amish quilts within the Lancaster tradition and the Midwest tradition. It is quilts from Pennsylvania and the hybrid forms from Illinois that appear to have a particular Welsh 'imprint.' But in the drama of their use of plain cloth and vibrant color combinations, all Amish quilts share with Welsh quilts a potent strength which has led to the construct of these quilts as powerful aesthetic objects.

Tying the Threads . . .

*I*T IS OVER THREE DECADES since the stylistic links between Amish and Welsh quilts were first documented. The notion that cultural cross-over between Amish and Welsh communities might explain the visual connections between the two quilt genres came just a little later, in the 1980s. Though debate inevitably ensued, discussions have remained largely informal and, for the most part, have not been grounded in any evidence base beyond the visual evidence within the quilts themselves. The questions of where such a cross-over might have occurred, or which direction cross-over could have taken, have until now remained unresolved. For this author, it has always seemed historically logical that cultural cross-over between Amish and Welsh communities was more likely to have occurred in the New World rather than in any part of Old World Europe or even, as has been suggested, on passage to America. Sustained contact through a coincidence of settlement patterns in the New World always seemed the most likely vector for cultural cross-over, rather than fleeting encounters in transient situations.

It was to find supporting evidence for this hypothesis that the researches on which this book is based began. And, indeed the evidence presented in the earlier chapters has shown that Amish and Welsh communities *did* live in close proximity in specific localities in nineteenth-century America, so it *was* possible for Welsh influence to have impacted on Amish quilt-making. Viewed from the perspective of historical geography, opportunity for social interaction between the Amish and Welsh certainly existed in nineteenth-century Pennsylvania and Ohio. Moreover, there was much common ground between nineteenth-century Amish and Welsh communities, most especially in their respective religious convictions. Both societies were strongly rooted in Protestant nonconformism with comparable systems of travelling ministers who maintained spiritual and social links between communities, particularly between communities with close family ties, such as the 'daughter' off-shoots from 'mother' communities. The research findings have also shown that, in their respective farm-centred activities, the Amish and the early nineteenth-century Welsh settlers shared a common economic base. Though the later nineteenth-century wave of industrial Welsh immigrants came initially to work in industry, some of this group also bought land to farm when they had acquired sufficient capital to do so.

As a consequence of these social, economic, and cultural connections, there was the potential for considerable empathy between Welsh and Amish communities. But there were possible barriers too, the most significant of which may have been that of language. Many Welsh immigrants spoke only Welsh, and Amish communities retained their Pennsylvanian German dialect, so interaction may have been inhibited until each community had a modicum of English language capability. But absorbing visual and technical competencies relies on observation, so verbal communication was not essential for cross-over in quilt-making.

The nature of Amish society in nineteenth-century America may also have contributed to closer interaction with non-Amish neighbors, particularly before the 1860s schisms which split the Amish church. However, the old Pennsylvania 'mother' communities tended towards the more conservative wing of the church, including the Somerset County group from which the Illinois Old Order Amish community sprang. The extent to which this may have become a factor in the development of the distinctive design style of the Lancaster quilts, and the eclectic mix of styles in the Illinois quilts, is for future research to determine. But it does raise a serious question as to whether the differing regional quilting styles found on Midwest and Lancaster Amish quilts relate to their respective 'change-minded' and 'tradition-minded' stances in the years of division that shook the Amish church between 1850 and 1878. It was a time of "remarkable disagreement, dissension, and schism among the Amish"[1] and, since it coincided with the early years of Amish quilt-making, the divisions may have impacted on this aspect of Amish culture in turn.

The social, economic, and cultural factors that linked contiguous Amish and Welsh societies in America in the nineteenth century argue for a level of social interaction that may have resulted in cultural cross-over. Bringing together the evidence that can be gleaned from surviving Amish and Welsh quilts with objective data from historical sources does give support for the theory of cross-over in quilt-making design, particularly in the relationships between Lancaster and Illinois Amish quilts with Welsh quilts. It would seem extraordinarily coincidental that two quilt styles with such close visual connections developed entirely independently in the nineteenth century, when—at that point in time—the communities within which these styles were common practice lived in geographic proximity to each other.

If there was cross-over in design style between Amish and Welsh quilts, however, the evidence is unequivocal about the direction the cross-over took. Making quilts in deep-dyed plain cloth pieced into large geometric shapes of abstract form was undoubtedly practised in Wales prior to the time that this dramatic style came into use for Amish quilts. Though there is ample evidence for growing American influence in Welsh (and wider British) quilt-making in the second half of the nineteenth century,[2] the characteristics of Welsh quilting were undoubtedly in place in the early years of the nineteenth century, as evidenced by surviving quilts from that time. In Wales, just as in other British regions, vernacular quilt-making evolved after the Industrial Revolution and developed into a visual tradition which held an ensemble of skill and knowledge. As designs and techniques were passed between the generations, quilt-makers in Wales responded to the local resource of an indigenous wool-manufacturing industry. This combination of cultural and economic forces shaped the design style of vernacular Welsh quilts, and the resulting style became, for Welsh quilt-makers, part of the aesthetic and cultural inheritance of their national society.

The extent to which this Welsh quilt-making inheritance influenced the development and design styles of classic Amish quilts is still opaque. But at each stage in the research undertaken for this book, the accumulation of objective data from a multi-disciplinary range of sources supported the subjective evidence contained within the quilts themselves. Taken as a whole, the weight of evidence suggests that the visual links between Amish and Welsh quilts are not accidental. It is entirely plausible that they could result from the absorption of characteristically Welsh elements of design style into historic Amish quilts when the two communities came together in nineteenth-century America. But the extent to which Welsh design style was absorbed across the full spectrum of Amish quilt-making seems to have been uneven, with Amish quilts in the Lancaster and broader Pennsylvanian traditions showing the closest parallels to Welsh quilts. Amish quilts in the Midwest tradition have strong affinities with nineteenth-century American quilt-making in terms of many of their pieced and quilted designs, but in their dramatic use of color and plain cloth they too relate to Welsh quilts.

That Amish and Welsh communities lived in close contiguity in nineteenth-century America is now established; identifying precise geographic localities where these two communities came together was a major objective of this research. But to build on the evidence base now laid down, locally-based archive searches in these localities will be required to progress the research agenda. If further insight is to be gained into Welsh influence on Amish quilt-making, and the inter-relationships between Amish and Welsh communities, it is most likely to come from in-depth studies of primary data sources in the localities where Amish and Welsh settlement paths crossed in nineteenth-century America.

And the quilts remain. As objects, they remain for further investigative and critical study, but they also remain as metaphors for the hidden paths of history and cultural connections that can be revealed when their 'seams' are unpicked and pried apart.

Endnotes

Introduction

1 In the context of this book, the term 'Amish' is used to denote groups in the Amish church that settled in the U.S. prior to the schisms of the 1860s and that, after the schisms, became the conservative wing of that church including the 'Old Order Amish.' The term 'Amish quilt' is used generically to include the quilts made by the pre-1860 Amish groups and later quilts made by the Old Order Amish and other conservative post-1860 Amish groups.

2 Hughes (1990) p. 14.

3 *Ibid.*, p. 23.

4 Haders (1976) p. 7.

5 Bishop and Safanda (1976) p. 15.

6 Grannick (1989) p. 34.

7 Diner (2002) p. 33.

8 Richardson and Griffiths (1977) p. 55.

9 Ron Simpson, Canadian quilt collector, and Joen Zinni, American quilt store owner and dealer, were both resident in London and acted as consultants to the programs, pers. comm. Ron Simpson, June 2008.

10 Osler (1987).

11 *Ibid,* p. 143.

12 Holstein (1996) p. 83.

13 For example, Lemon (1972), Erickson (1976), Erickson (1989), and Van Vugt (1999).

14 Van Vugt (1999) p. 4.

15 Prichard (2010).

Chapter 1

1 Holstein (1991) p. 30.

2 *Ibid.*, p. 43.

3 Haders (1976), Bishop and Safander (1976).

4 Schmucker (2006).
5 Haders (1976) p. 7.
6 Herr (1996) pp. 55–57.
7 Schmucker (2009).
8 Herr (1996) p. 46.
9 Grannick (1989) p. 23.
10 *Ibid.*, p. 25.
11 Shaw (2009) p. 32.

Chapter 2

1 Osler (1987) p. 158.
2 Sessions Papers, Anglesey Quarter Sessions, Ref: WQ/S/1815/H/14, December 28 1814, Anglesey (Ynys Mon) Record Office, Llangefni.
3 Sessions Papers, Anglesey Quarter Sessions, Ref: Q/A/G/687, September 19 1829, Anglesey (Ynys Mon) Record Office, Llangefni.
4 Sessions Papers, Anglesey Quarter Sessions, Ref: WQ/S/1816/T/22, June 1 1816, Anglesey (Ynys Mon) Record Office, Llangefni.
5 Sessions Papers, Anglesey Quarter Sessions, Ref: WQ/S/1821/T/206, April 12 1821, Anglesey (Ynys Mon) Record Office, Llangefni.
6 Memorandum of Recognizance, Ref: XQS/1755/57, July 7 1755, Gwynedd Archives, Caernarfon.
7 Parry Jones (1948) p. 87.
8 Pers. comm., email from Jen Jones, Nov 3 2010.
9 FitzRandolph (1954) p. 34.
10 *Ibid.*
11 Jenkins, J. G. (1969) p. 97.
12 Thomas Martyn, unpublished manuscript, NLW MS 1340C, p. 150, National Library of Wales, Aberystwyth.
13 Stevens (2002) p. 63.
14 Borrow (1862) p. 379.
15 Dyer's Notebook, NLW MS 2865A, National Library of Wales, Aberystwyth.
16 Dyer's Notebook, NLW MS 901A, National Library of Wales, Aberystwyth.
17 Schmucker (2009) p. 24.

Chapter 3
1 Stoltzfus (1958) p. 240.
2 *Ibid.*, p. 251.
3 Crowley (1978) pp. 249–64.
4 Bender (2010).
5 Beachy (1958) p. 267.
6 Data compiled by the author from U.S. Census 1800, Somerset County Pennsylvania, Quamahoning Township. Accessed at: http://censusfinder.com/pennsylvania_census5.htm, October 2008. Full statistical summations included in "The Spatial

Distribution of Amish and Welsh Settlements in Nineteenth-century Pennsylvania: Implications for Cultural Cross-over in Quiltmaking," unpublished paper presented to 4th Biennale Symposium *The Global Quilt: Cultural Contexts*, International Quilt Study Center & Museum, University of Nebraska–Lincoln, April 2009.

7 Data compiled by the author from U.S. Census: 1800; 1810; 1820; and 1850. Somerset County Pennsylvania, Conemaugh Township. Access and presentation as note 6, above.
8 Beachy (1958) pp. 283-84.
9 *Ibid.*, p. 292.
10 Crowley (1978) Fig. 3.
11 *Ibid.*, pp. 253–54.
12 Nolt (1992) p. 122.
13 *Ibid.*, p.142.
14 *Ibid.*, pp. 80–81.
15 Scott (1986) p. 18.
16 Schlabach (1988) p. 22.
17 Yoder (1987) p. 95.
18 Nolt (1992) p. 172.
19 Grannick (1989) pp. 30–31.
20 *Ibid.*, p. 106.
21 Holstein (1996) p. 98.
22 Keller (2001).
23 Grannick (1989) p. 29.
24 Wass (2004), pp. 153–54.
25 Grannick (1989) p. 25.
26 Lasansky (1985a) p. 27.
27 Lasansky (1985b) pp. 85–93.
28 Fischer (1989) pp. 605–781.
29 Grannick (1989) p. 25.

Chapter 4
1 Letter, dated October 14, 1817, from David Shone Harry (David Jones), joiner, settled in Albany, New York, to his wife in Llwyngwril, North Wales, quoted in Conway (1961) p. 56.
2 Conway (1974) p. 219.
3 Dodd (1958).
4 *Ibid.*
5 Thomas (1852) p. 29.
6 Magda (1986).
7 Eppihimer (1983) p. 5; *see* Mast and Simpson (1942) p. 463.
8 Thomas (1872) p. 22.
9 Van Vugt (1999) p. 96.
10 Hartman (1983).
11 Data compiled by the author from U.S. Census 1850, Cambria County Pennsylvania. Accessed at: http://censusfinder.com/pennsylvania_census5.

htm, October 2008. Full statistical summations as in Chapter 3, note 6.

12 Jones, W. D. (1993), p. xx [Introduction].
13 Thomas (1872).
14 Jones, W. H. (1907).
15 Estimated from Berthoff (1953) p. 5.
16 Erickson (1989).
17 Conway (1961) pp. 22–23.
18 Davies, P. G. (1981) p. 341.
19 Gifford and Greenhill (1973) p. 10.
20 *Ibid.*, p. 146.
21 Murray, J.B. (1843), Merseyside Maritime Museum, Liverpool, DX/520/2.
22 Conway (1961) p. 60.
23 Data in unpublished document by Barbara Brackman for the Lyon County (Kansas) Historical Society, March 1992; subsequent family history data from the quilt's donor, John Atherton, email to author March 9 2005.
24 Gero (2000) p. 7.
25 Robson and MacDonald (1995) p. 24.

Chapter 5

1 Jones, W. D. (1993) pp. 250–51.
2 Egle (1876) pp. 461–78.
3 Data compiled by the author from U.S. Census 1800, Somerset County Pennsylvania, Cambria Township and Quamahoning Township. Accessed at: http://censusfinder.com/pennsylvania_census5.htm October 2008. Full statistical summations as in Chapter 3, note 6.
4 Data compiled by the author from U.S. Census: 1800; 1810; 1820; 1850. Somerset County Pennsylvania, Conemaugh Township. Access and presentation as note 3, above.
5 Data compiled by the author from U.S. Census: 1800; 1810; 1820; 1850 for Somerset County Pennsylvania, Cambria Township. Access and presentation as note 3, above.

6 Magda (1986).
7 Thomas (1872) p. 22.
8 Ellis and Evans (1883) p. 862.
9 Data compiled by the author from U.S. Census 1850, York County Pennsylvania, Peachbottom Township. Access and presentation as note 3, above.
10 Ellis and Evans (1883) p. 860.
11 Data compiled by the author from U.S. Census 1850, Lancaster County Pennsylvania, Fulton Township, consulted at Lancaster: Lancaster County Historical Society. Full statistical summations as in Chapter 3, note 6.
12 Thomas (1872) p. 34.
13 Smucker (1880a) available at: http://ohio.llgc.org.uk/erth-lick-h.php. Accessed August 5 2010.
14 Smucker (1880b) access as note 13, above.
15 Email to Ellen Endslow, Chester County Historical Society, from Pam Shenk, Pottstown, Pennsylvania. Forwarded to author by Pam Shenk, January 6 2004.

Chapter 6

1 Herr (2004) p. 22.
2 Wass (2004) p. 16.
3 Herr (1996) pp. 55–57.
4 Nolt (1992) p. 172.
5 Schmucker (2009) p. 17.
6 Shaw (2009) p. 36.
7 Haders (1976) pp. 26–27.
8 Osler (1987) plates 5 & 6; Osler (2000) pp. 38–41.
9 Hughes (1990) p. 23.

Chapter 7

1 Nolt (1992) p. 158.
2 Osler (2006); Osler (2010) p. 117.

Bibliography

Adamson, Jeremy. *Calico and Chintz: Antique Quilts from the Collection of Patricia S. Smith.* Washington, DC: Smithsonian Institution (Renwick Gallery), 1997.

Baines, Dudley. *Emigration from Europe, 1815–1930, New Studies in Economic and Social History.* Cambridge: Cambridge University Press, 1995.

———. "Regional Emigration from Britain 1815–1939: Comparisons and Contexts," in *Regional Perspectives on Emigration from the British Isles,* proceedings of Research Day School, pp. 7-30. Liverpool: University of Liverpool/National Museums and Galleries on Merseyside, March 1996.

Beachy, Alvin J. "The Amish Settlement in Somerset County, Pennsylvania," *Mennonite Quarterly Review,* 28, October 1958, pp. 263–92.

Bender, Harold S. "Amish Mennonites," *Global Anabaptist Mennonite Encyclopedia Online* (1953). Accessed August 4 2010: http://www.gameo.org/encyclopedia/contents/A4594ME.html

Berthoff, Rowland. *British Immigrants in Industrial America.* Cambridge, Massachussetts: Harvard University Press, 1953.

———. "Welsh", in Thernstrom, S. (Ed) *Harvard Encyclopedia of American Ethnic Groups,* pp. 1011–17. Cambridge, Massachusetts: Harvard University Press, 1980.

Bishop, Robert. *New Discoveries in American Quilts.* New York: E.P. Dutton Inc, 1975.

——— and Safanda, Elizabeth, *A Gallery of Amish Quilts.* New York: E.P. Dutton, 1976.

Borrow, George. *Wild Wales.* London: Dent, 1958 (first published 1862).

Coleman, Terry. *Passage to America.* London: Hutchinson & Co., 1972.

Conway, Alan. *The Welsh in America: Letters from the Immigrants.* Cardiff: University of Wales Press, 1961.

———. *Welsh Emigration to the United States.* Cambridge, Massachusetts: Harvard University Press, 1974.

Crowley, William J. "Old Order Amish Settlement: Diffusion and Growth," *Annals of the Association of American Geographers*, 66(2), 1978, pp. 249–64.

Davies, John. *A History of Wales*. London: Allen Lane/ Penguin, 1990.

Davies, Phillips G. (Transl). "The State of Pennsylvania: From Bromley and Jones, Instructions for the Immigrant," *Pennsylvania History*, 1, 48(4), October 1981, pp. 335–46.

Diner, Hasier R, "Insights and Blind Spots: Writing History from Inside and Outside", in Schmidt, Kimberly D. *et al.* (Eds). *Strangers at Home: Amish and Mennonite Women in History*. Baltimore, Maryland: The Johns Hopkins University Press, 2002.

Dodd, A. H. "The Background of the Welsh Quaker Migration to Pennsylvania," *Journal of the Merioneth Historical and Record Society*, 3(2), 1958.

———. *Industrial Revolution in North Wales*. Cardiff: University of Wales Press, 1971.

Egle, William D. *An Illustrated History of the Commonwealth of Pennsylvania*. Harrisburg, Pennsylvania: DeWitt C. Goodrich & Co, 1876.

Ellis, Franklin and Evans, Samuel. *History of Lancaster County, Pennsylvania*. Philadelphia: Everts & Peck, 1883.

Eppihimer, Margaret P. *Headwaters of the Brandywine..., A History of Honey Brook County*. Honey Brook County, Pennsylvania: Honey Brook County Board of Supervisors, 1983.

Erickson, Charlotte. *Emigration from Europe 1815–1914: Select Documents*. London: Adam & Charles Black, 1976.

———. "English Women Emigrants in America in the Nineteenth Century: Expectations and Reality," *Fawcett Library Papers No. 7*. London: LLRS Publications, 1983.

———. "Emigration from the British Isles to the U.S.A. in 1841, Part 1, Emigration from the British Isles," *Population Studies*, 43, 1989, 347-67.

———. *Leaving England: Essays on British Emigration in the Nineteenth Century*. Ithaca, New York: Cornell University Press, 1994.

———. "The United States Passenger Lists," in *Regional Perspectives on Emigration from the British Isles*, proceedings of Research Day School, pp. 31–48. Liverpool: University of Liverpool/National Museums and Galleries on Merseyside, March 1996.

Fischer, David Hackett. *Albion's Seed: Four British Folkways in America*. New York/Oxford: Oxford University Press, 1989.

FitzRandolph, Mavis. *Traditional Quilting*. London: Batsford, 1954.

Gero, Annette. *Historic Australian Quilts*. New South Wales: National Trust of Australia/Beagle Press, 2000.

Gifford, Ann and Greenhill, Basil. *Women Under Sail*. Newton Abbot, Devon: David & Charles, 1973.

Grannick, Eve Wheatcroft. *The Amish Quilt*. Intercourse, Pennsylvania: Good Books, 1989.

Gwyn, David. *Gwynedd: Inheriting a Revolution. The Archaeology of Industrialisation in North-West Wales*. Chichester: Phillimore Press, 2006.

Haders, Phyllis, *Sunshine and Shadow: The Amish and Their Quilts*. New York: Universe Books, 1976.

Hartman, Edward George. *Americans from Wales*. New York: Octagon Books, 1983.

Herr, Patricia. "Quilts Within the Amish Culture," in *A Quiet Spirit: Amish Quilts from the Collection of Cindy Tietze & Stuart Hodosh*, exhibition catalogue, pp. 45–67. Los Angeles: UCLA Fowler Museum of Cultural History, 1996.

———. *Amish Arts of Lancaster County*. Atglen, Pennsylvania: Schiffer Publishing Ltd, 1998.

———. *Quilting Traditions: Pieces from the Past*. Atglen, Pennsylvania: Schiffer Publishing Ltd, 2000.

———. *Amish Quilts of Lancaster County*. Atglen, Pennsylvania: Schiffer Publishing Ltd, 2004.

Holstein, Jonathan. *The Pieced Quilt: An American Design Tradition*. Boston: Little, Brown & Co. 1973.

———. *Abstract Design in American Quilts: A Biography of an Exhibition*. Louisville, Kentucky: The Kentucky Quilt Project Inc., 1991.

———. "In Plain Sight: The Aesthetics of Amish Quilts," in *A Quiet Spirit: Amish Quilts from the Collection of Cindy Tietze & Stuart Hodosh*, exhibition catalogue, pp. 69–121. Los Angeles: UCLA Fowler Museum of Cultural History, 1996.

Hostetler, John A. *Amish Society*, 4th edition. Baltimore/ London: The Johns Hopkins University Press, 1993.

Hufnagel, Florian (Ed). *Diamonds and Bars: Die Kunst der Amish/The Art of the Amish People*. Stuttgart/New York: Arnoldsche Art Publishers, 2007.

Hughes, Robert. *The Art of the Quilt*. New York: Callaway Editions, 1990/London: Phaidon Press, 1994.

Jenkins, J. Geraint. *The Welsh Woollen Industry*. Cardiff: National Museum of Wales/Welsh Folk Museum, 1969.
———. *The Flannel Makers: A Brief History of the Welsh Woollen Industry*. Conwy: Gwasg Carreg Gwalch, 2005.

Jenkins, Mary and Claridge, Clare. *Making Welsh Quilts: The Textile Tradition that Inspired the Amish?* Newton Abbot, Devon: David & Charles, 2005.

Jones, Aled and Jones, Bill. *Welsh Reflections: Y Drych & America, 1851–2001*. Llandysul, Ceredigion: Gomer Press, 2001.

Jones, Anna M. *The Rural Industries of England and Wales: A Survey Made on Behalf of the Agricultural Economics Research Institute*, vol. 4, Wales. Oxford: Clarendon Press, 1927.

Jones, Bill. "Language and Identity in Welsh Migrant Communities in the United States During the Late 19th and Early 20th Centuries," in *Regional Perspectives on Emigration from the British Isles,* proceedings of Research Day School, pp. 121–40. Liverpool: University of Liverpool/National Museums and Galleries on Merseyside, March 1996.

Jones, Jen. *Welsh Quilts, a Towy guide*. Carmarthen: Towy Publishing, 1997.
———. *Les Quilts Gallois/Welsh Quilts*. Saint Etienne de Montluc: Quiltmania, 2005.

Jones, R. Merfyn and Lovecy, Jill. "Slate Workers in Wales, France and the United States. A Comparative Study," *Industrial Gwynedd*, vol. 3, 1998.

Jones, William D. *Wales in America: Scranton and the Welsh, 1860-1920,* Studies in Welsh History 8. Cardiff/Scranton: University of Wales Press/University of Scranton Press, 1993.

Jones, William Harvey. "Welsh Settlements in Ohio," *The Cambrian* (1907), vol 27, nos. 7-9, pp. 311-17, pp. 344–50, pp. 395-99.

Keller, Patricia J. "The Quilts of Lancaster County, Pennsylvania: Production, Context and Meaning, 1750-1884." Ph.D. dissertation, University of Delaware, 2007.

Kollmorgen, Walter. *Culture of a Contemporary Rural Community: The Old Order Amish of Lancaster County, Pennsylvania, Rural Life Studies 4*. Washington, DC: US Department of Agriculture, 1942.

Knowles, Anne Kelly. "Immigrant Trajectories through the Rural–Industrial Transition in Wales and the United States, 1795-1850," *Annals of the Association of American Geographers*, 85(2), 1995, pp. 246–66.

———. "Religious Identity as Ethnic Identity," in Ostergren, Robert C. and Vale, Thomas R. (Eds) *Wisconsin Land and Life*, pp. 282–89. Madison, Wisconsin: University of Wisconsin Press, 1997.
———. "Migration, Nationalism and the Construction of Welsh Identity," in Herb, G. H. and Kaplan, D. (Eds) *Nested Identities: Nationalism, Territory and Scale*. Lanham, Maryland: Rowman & Littlefield, 1999.

Lasansky, Jeanette. *In the Heart of Pennsylvania: 19th and 20th Century Quiltmaking Traditions*. Lewisburg, Pennsylvania: Union County Historical Society Oral Traditions Project, 1985.
———. "The Role of Haps in Central Pennsylvania's 19th and 20th Century Quiltmaking Traditions," *Uncoverings*, vol. 6, 1985, pp. 85–93.

Lemon, James T. *The Best Poor Man's Country: A Geographical Study of Early Southeastern Pennsylvania*. Baltimore, Maryland: The Johns Hopkins University Press, 1972.

Magda, Matthew S. *The Welsh in Pennsylvania, The Peoples of Pennsylvania*, Pamphlet No. 2. Harrisburg, Pennsylvania: Pennsylvania Historical and Museum Commission, 1986.

Mast, C. Z. and Simpson, Robert E. *Annals of the Conestoga Valley in Lancaster, Berks and Chester Counties, Pennsylvania*. Elverson/Churchtown, Pennsylvania: Mast & Simpson, 1942.

Merseyside Maritime Museum. "Emigration to USA and Canada," *Maritime Archives and Library*, Sheet No. 13. Merseyside Maritime Museum, Liverpool.
———. "Liverpool and Emigration in the 19th and 20th Centuries," *Maritime Archives and Library,* Sheet No. 64. Merseyside Maritime Museum, Liverpool.

Murray, J. Buxton, *A New Guide for Emigrants to the Western States of North America*. Glasgow: J. Buxton Murray, 1843 (Merseyside Maritime Museum, Liverpool, DX/520/2).

Nolt, Steven M. *A History of the Amish*. Intercourse, Pennsylvania: Good Books, 1992.

Osler, Dorothy. *Traditional British Quilts*. London: Batsford, 1987.
———. *North Country Quilts: Legends and Living Tradition*, Barnard Castle, Co. Durham: The Bowes Museum, 2000.
———. "Across the Pond: New World Influences on Old World Traditions," *Quilters Newsletter Magazine*, June 2006, pp. 38–41.

———. "Maintaining the Craft: British Quilt-making 1900–45," in Prichard, Sue (Ed) *Quilts 1700-2010: Hidden Histories, Untold Stories*. London: V&A Publishing, 2010.

Parry Jones, D. *Welsh Country Upbringing*. London: Batsford, 1948.

Pottinger, David. *Quilts from the Indiana Amish: A Regional Collection*. New York: E.P. Dutton Inc, 1983.

Prichard, Sue (Ed). *Quilts 1700-2010: Hidden Histories, Untold Stories*. London: V&A Publishing, 2010.

Richardson, Rosamund and Griffiths, Erica. *Discovering Patchwork*. London: BBC Publications, 1977.

Robson, Scott and MacDonald, Sharon. *Old Nova Scotian Quilts*. Halifax: Nova Scotia Museum/Nimbus Publishing, 1995.

Schlabach, Theron F. *Peace, Faith, Nation: Mennonites and Amish in Nineteenth-century America*. Scottdale, Pennsylvania: Herald Press, 1988.

Schmidt, Kimberly D., Umble, Diane Zimmerman, and Reschly, Steven D. (Eds). *Strangers at Home: Amish and Mennonite Women in History*. Baltimore/London: The Johns Hopkins University Press (2002).

Schmucker, Janneken. "Destination Amish Country: The Consumption of Quilts in Lancaster County, Pennsylvania," *Mennonite Quarterly Review*, April 2006, pp. 185–206.

———. "Quilts in Amish Contexts: Traditions and Adaptations" in *Amish Abstractions: Quilts from the Collection of Stephen and Faith Brown*, exhibition catalogue, pp. 11–27. San Francisco: Fine Arts Museums of San Francisco/Pomegranate Communications, 2009.

Scott, Stephen. *Why Do They Dress That Way?* People's Place Booklet No. 7. Intercourse, Pennsylvania: Good Books, 1986.

Shaw, Robert. "Fundamentally Abstract: The Aesthetic Achievement of Amish Quiltmakers," in *Amish Abstractions: Quilts from the Collection of Stephen and Faith Brown*, exhibition catalogue, pp. 29–37. San Francisco: Fine Arts Museums of San Francisco/Pomegranate Communications, 2009.

Skeel, Caroline A. J. "The Welsh Woollen Industry in the Eighteenth and Nineteenth Centuries," *Archaeologia Cambrensis*, 79 (1), June, 1924, pp. 1–38.

Smith Futhey, F. J. and Cope, Gilbert. *History of Chester County, Pennsylvania*, Parts 1 & 2. Philadelphia: Louis H. Everts, 1881.

Smucker, Isaac. "Historical Sketch of the Welsh Hills, Licking County," *The Cambrian*, vol. 1(2) 1880, pp. 46-53.

———. "Historical Sketch of the Welsh Hills, Licking County," *The Cambrian*, vol. 1(3) 1880, pp. 81–86.

Stevens, Christine. *Quilts*. Llandysul: Gomer Press/National Museum of Wales, 1993.

———. "Welsh Peasant Dress: Workwear or National Costume?" *Textile History* 33(1), 2002.

Stoltzfus, Grant M. "History of the First Amish Mennonite Communities in America," *Mennonite Quarterly Review*, 28, October 1958, pp. 235–62.

Thomas, Rev. R. D. (Iorthryn Gwynedd), *America or Miscellaneous Notes on the United States Useful for Emigrants* (compiled 1852), transl. by T. I. Ellis, C. Taylor (Ed), NLW MS 9521A. Aberystwyth: National Library of Wales, 1973.

———. *A History of the Welsh in America*, (originally published 1872), transl. Phillips G. Davies. Lanham, New York/London: University Press of America, 1983.

Trifanoff, Karen M. "Amish Culture as preserved in Quilts," *Journal of Cultural Geography*, vol. 10 (1), September 1989, pp. 63–73.

Van Vugt, William E. *Britain to America: Mid-Nineteenth Century Immigrants to the United States*. Urbana, Illinois: University of Illinois Press, 1999.

Wass, Janice Tauer. *Illinois Amish Quilts: Sharing Threads of Tradition*. Springfield, Illinois: Illinois State Museum, 2004.

Wilson, Roger B., Robinson, Donald C., Morris, James L., and Glenn, David B. *The River and the Ridge: 300 Years of Local History, Peach Bottom Township and Delta, Pennsylvania, Cardiff and Whiteford, Maryland*. Baltimore, Maryland: Gateway Press, 2003.

Yoder, Paton. *Tennessee John Stoltzfus: Amish Church-Related Documents and Family Letters*. Lancaster, Pennsylvania: Lancaster Mennonite Historical Society, 1987.

Index

Entries that relate to figures are given in bold.